KNITTING UNDER STRAND

Insert right needle under loose strand and knit next stitch on left needle, pulling stitch under strand (**Fig. 2**).

Fig. 2

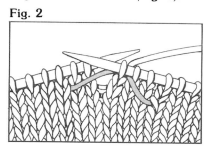

SSK

With yarn to the back of work, separately slip two stitches as if to **knit** (**Fig. 3a**). Insert **left** needle to the **front** through both stitches (**Fig. 3b**). Knit together (**Fig. 3c**).

Fig. 3a

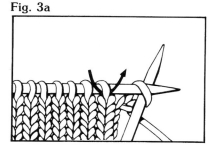

Fig. 3b

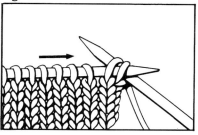

Fig. 3c

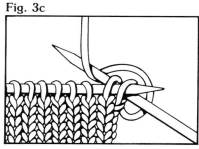

SINGLE CROCHET

Insert hook in next stitch or in end of next row and pull up a loop, YO and draw through both loops on hook (**Fig. 4**) (**single crochet made, abbreviated sc**).

Fig. 4

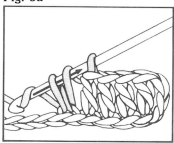

DOUBLE CROCHET

YO, insert hook in stitch or in chain and pull up a loop, YO and draw through 2 loops on hook (**Fig. 5a**), YO and draw through remaining 2 loops on hook (**Fig. 5b**) (**double crochet made, abbreviated dc**).

Fig. 5a

Fig. 5b

We have made every effort to ensure that these instructions are accurate and complete. We cannot, however, be responsible for human error, typographical mistakes, or variations in individual work.

Afghans made and instructions tested by Lissa Amman, Joan Beebe, Jo Ann Bowling, Rhona Czepiel, Liz Edmondson, Suzan Gibson, Raymelle Greening, Kathleen Harper, Lisa Hightower, Shala Johnson, Terry Kimbrough, Kay Meadors, Lois Phillips, Kitty Jo Pietzuch, Donna Soellner, and Laurie Terpstra.

Sampler Afghan

Finished Size: Approximately 48" x 60"

MATERIALS
Worsted Weight Yarn, approximately:
57 ounces, (1,620 grams, 3,825 yards)
Straight knitting needles, size 8 (5.00 mm) **or** size needed for gauge
Crochet hook, size H (5.00 mm)
Yarn needle

GAUGE: In Stockinette Stitch,
18 sts and 24 rows = 4"

Each Afghan consists of 20 squares. You can arrange your squares at random or in a planned pattern.
If you want to duplicate our cover Afghans exactly, follow the Assembly Diagrams on page 4. There is a blank diagram for your own arrangement.

Make 20 squares of your choice following instructions on pages 5-30. As you complete each square, label it with its corresponding number for ease in placement at assembly.

FINISHING
BLOCKING
Due to the variety of pattern stitches used, some of the squares may benefit from being blocked to the proper size. Place each square on a clean terry towel over a flat surface (each square should measure 12" before edging is added); pin in place using rust-proof pins where needed. Steam lightly and allow to dry **completely**.

ASSEMBLY
Afghan is assembled by joining 5 completed squares into 4 vertical strips and then by joining strips.
Lay out squares in desired order.
Join squares as follows:
With **right** sides together, insert yarn needle from **right** to **left** through **front** loop of first square and **back** loop of second square *(Fig. 6)*. Bring the needle around and insert it from **right** to **left** through the next loop on both squares.
Continue in this manner, keeping the sewing yarn fairly loose.

Fig. 6

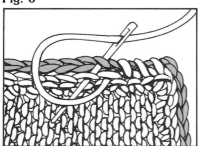

BORDER
Method #1
With **right** side facing, join yarn with slip st in any corner; ch 1, sc evenly around Afghan working 3 sc in each corner; join with slip st to first sc, finish off.

Method #2
Round 1: With **right** side facing, join yarn with slip st in top right corner; ch 1, ★ 3 sc in corner, work 197 sc evenly spaced across to next corner, 3 sc in corner, work 249 sc evenly spaced across to next corner; repeat from ★ once **more**; join with slip st to first sc: 904 sc.
Round 2: Slip st in next sc, ch 7, dc in fourth ch from hook *(Figs. 5a & b, page 2)*, dc in same sc, skip next 3 sc, ★ (dc, ch 4, dc in fourth ch from hook, dc) in next sc, skip next 3 sc; repeat from ★ around; join with slip st to third ch of beginning ch-7, finish off.

ASSEMBLY DIAGRAMS

Sampler #1

4	43	47	3
42	22	23	25
17	29	48	46
10	37	52	21
60	16	59	12

Sampler #2

55	41	56	26
13	51	44	20
5	14	53	38
57	24	1	49
54	50	58	19

Sampler #3

9	39	11	27
34	45	31	15
28	8	18	35
32	6	30	2
7	36	33	40

Your Arrangement

4

1. Eyelet Butterflies

Cast on 54 sts.
Row 1: Purl across.
Note: When instructed to slip a stitch, always slip as if to **knit**.
Row 2 (Right side): K 12, K2 tog, YO *(Fig. 1a, page 1)*, K5, K2 tog, YO, K4, K2 tog, slip 1, K1, PSSO, K4, YO, K2 tog, K5, YO, K2 tog, K 12: 52 sts.
Row 3: P 14, YO *(Fig. 1d, page 1)*, P2 tog, P 20, P2 tog, YO, P 14.
Row 4: K 12, K2 tog, YO, K5, K2 tog, YO, K3, K2 tog, YO 3 times, slip 1, K1, PSSO, K3, YO, K2 tog, K5, YO, K2 tog, K 12: 53 sts.
Row 5: P 14, YO, P2 tog, P9, drop 3 YOs off left needle, P9, P2 tog, YO, P 14: 50 sts.
Row 6: K 12, K2 tog, YO, K5, K2 tog, YO, K2, K2 tog, YO 3 times, slip 1, K1, PSSO, K2, YO, K2 tog, K5, YO, K2 tog, K 12: 51 sts.
Row 7: P 14, YO, P2 tog, P8, drop 3 YOs off left needle, P8, P2 tog, YO, P 14: 48 sts.
Row 8: K 12, K2 tog, YO, K5, K2 tog, YO, K1, K2 tog, YO 4 times, slip 1, K1, PSSO, K1, YO, K2 tog, K5, YO, K2 tog, K 12: 50 sts.
Row 9: P 14, YO, P2 tog, P7, drop 4 YOs off left needle, P7, P2 tog, YO, P 14: 46 sts.
Row 10: K 12, K2 tog, YO, K5, K2 tog, YO, K2 tog, turn work, add on 5 sts *(Figs. 8a & b)*, turn work, insert right needle under 6 horizontal strands, YO and draw up a st *(Fig. 7)*, place st on left needle and knit this st, turn work, add on 4 sts, turn work, slip 1, K1, PSSO, YO, K2 tog, K5, YO, K2 tog, K 12: 54 sts.

Fig. 7

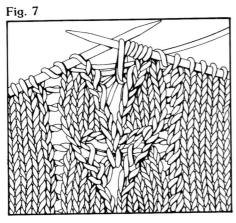

Row 11: P 14, YO, P2 tog, P 22, P2 tog, YO, P 14.
Repeat Rows 2-11 until square measures approximately 12″ from cast on edge, ending by working Row 11.
Bind off all sts leaving last loop on needle.
Edging: Drop loop from needle, insert crochet hook in loop, do **not** turn; work 3 sc in each corner and 48 sc evenly spaced across each side *(Fig. 4, page 2)*; join with slip st to first sc, finish off.

ADDING ON STITCHES

Insert right needle into stitch as if to knit, yarn over and pull loop through *(Fig. 8a)*, slip loop just worked back onto left needle *(Fig. 8b)*. Repeat for required number of stitches.

Fig. 8a

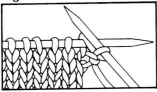

Fig. 8b

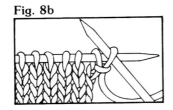

2. Eyelet Diamond and Cables

Additional materials: Cable needle

Note: When instructed to slip a stitch, always slip as if to **knit**.

Cast on 63 sts.
Row 1 AND ALL WRONG SIDE ROWS: K1, P1, K1, P6, K1, (P1, K1) twice, P6, K1, (P1, K1) 3 times, P9, K1, (P1, K1) 3 times, P6, K1, (P1, K1) twice, P6, K1, P1, K1.
Row 2 (Right side): K1, P1, K1, work Cable as follows: slip 3 sts onto cable needle and hold in **front** of work, K3, K3 from cable needle **(Cable made)**, K1, (P1, K1) twice, work Cable, (K1, P1) 3 times, K3, K2 tog, YO *(Fig. 1a, page 1)*, K1, YO, slip 1, K1, PSSO, K3, (P1, K1) 3 times, work Cable, K1, (P1, K1) twice, work Cable, K1, P1, K1.
Row 4: (K1, P1, K8, P1) twice, (K1, P1) twice, K2, K2 tog, YO, K3, YO, slip 1, K1, PSSO, K2, (P1, K1) twice, (P1, K8, P1, K1) twice.
Row 6: (K1, P1, K8, P1) twice, K1, (P1, K1) twice, K2 tog, YO, K5, YO, slip 1, K1, PSSO, K1, (P1, K1) twice, (P1, K8, P1, K1) twice.
Row 8: K1, P1, K1, work Cable, K1, (P1, K1) twice, work Cable, (K1, P1) 3 times, K2, YO, slip 1, K1, PSSO, K3, K2 tog, YO, K2, (P1, K1) 3 times, work Cable, K1, (P1, K1) twice, work Cable, K1, P1, K1.
Row 10: (K1, P1, K8, P1) twice, (K1, P1) twice, K3, YO, slip 1, K1, PSSO, K1, K2 tog, YO, K3, (P1, K1) twice, (P1, K8, P1, K1) twice.
Row 12: (K1, P1, K8, P1) twice, (K1, P1) twice, K4, YO, slip 1, K2 tog, PSSO, YO, K4, (P1, K1) twice, (P1, K8, P1, K1) twice.
Row 14: Repeat Row 2.
Row 16: Repeat Row 4.
Row 18: Repeat Row 6.
Row 20: (K1, P1, K8, P1) twice, (K1, P1) twice, K2, YO, slip 1, K1, PSSO, K3, K2 tog, YO, K2, (P1, K1) twice, (P1, K8, P1, K1) twice.
Row 22: Repeat Row 10.
Row 24: Repeat Row 12.
Repeat Rows 1-24 until square measures approximately 12″ from cast on edge, ending by working a **wrong** side row.
Bind off all sts leaving last loop on needle.
Edging: Drop loop from needle, insert crochet hook in loop, do **not** turn; work 3 sc in each corner and 48 sc evenly spaced across each side *(Fig. 4, page 2)*; join with slip st to first sc, finish off.

3. Hunter's Stitch

Cast on 70 sts.
Row 1 (Right side): P4, ★ K1 tbl, (P1, K1 tbl) 3 times, P4; repeat from ★ across.
Row 2: K4, ★ P1, (K1 tbl, P1) 3 times, K4; repeat from ★ across.
Repeat Rows 1 and 2 until square measures approximately 12″ from cast on edge, ending by working Row 1.
Bind off all sts leaving last loop on needle.
Edging: Drop loop from needle, insert crochet hook in loop, turn; work 3 sc in each corner and 48 sc evenly spaced across each side *(Fig. 4, page 2)*; join with slip st to first sc, finish off.

4. Semi-Woven Lattice

Cast on 54 sts.
Rows 1-9: Knit across.
Row 10 (Right side): K6, P3, K2, (P 13, K2) twice, P7, K6.
Note: When instructed to slip a stitch, always slip as if to **purl**, with yarn held in front (on the wrong side).
Row 11: K5, slip 1, K7, P2, (K 13, P2) twice, K3, slip 1, K5.
Row 12: K6, P3, K2, (P 13, K2) twice, P7, K6.
Row 13: K5, slip 1, P 42, slip 1, K5.
Row 14: K6, P1, K1, P1, K2, P2, K2, ★ P1, (K1, P1) 4 times, K2, P2, K2; repeat from ★ once **more**, P1, K1, P1, K6.
Row 15: K5, slip 1, K1, P1, K1, P2, K2, P2, ★ K1, (P1, K1) 4 times, P2, K2, P2; repeat from ★ once **more**, K1, P1, K1, slip 1, K5.
Row 16: K7, P1, K3, P2, K3, ★ P1, (K1, P1) 3 times, K3, P2, K3; repeat from ★ once **more**, P1, K7.
Row 17: K5, slip 1, P1, K1, P3, K2, P3, ★ K1, (P1, K1) 3 times, P3, K2, P3; repeat from ★ once **more**, K1, P1, slip 1, K5.
Rows 18-23: Repeat Rows 14-17 once, then repeat Rows 14 and 15 once **more**.
Row 24: K6, P7, K2, (P 13, K2) twice, P3, K6.
Row 25: K5, slip 1, K3, P2, (K 13, P2) twice, K7, slip 1, K5.
Row 26: K6, P7, K2, (P 13, K2) twice, P3, K6.
Row 27: K5, slip 1, P 42, slip 1, K5.
Rows 28-63: Repeat Rows 10-27 twice.
Rows 64-71: Knit across.
Bind off all sts leaving last loop on needle.
Edging: Drop loop from needle, insert crochet hook in loop, do **not** turn; work 3 sc in each corner and 48 sc evenly spaced across each side *(Fig. 4, page 2)*; join with slip st to first sc, finish off.

5. Double Parallelogram

Cast on 54 sts.
Row 1 (Right side): K2, (P5, K5) 5 times, P2.
Row 2: K3, (P5, K5) 5 times, P1.
Row 3: (P5, K5) 5 times, P4.
Row 4: (K5, P5) 5 times, K4.
Row 5: P3, (K5, P5) 5 times, K1.
Row 6: K1, (P5, K5) 5 times, P3.
Row 7: K4, (P5, K5) 5 times.
Row 8: P4, (K5, P5) 5 times.
Row 9: P1, (K5, P5) 5 times, K3.
Row 10: P2, (K5, P5) 5 times, K2.
Repeat Rows 1-10 until square measures approximately 12″ from cast on edge, ending by working a **right** side row.
Bind off all sts leaving last loop on needle.
Edging: Drop loop from needle, insert crochet hook in loop, turn; work 3 sc in each corner and 48 sc evenly spaced across each side *(Fig. 4, page 2)*; join with slip st to first sc, finish off.

6. Harris Tweed Pattern

Cast on 60 sts.
Rows 1-3: (K3, P3) 10 times.
Row 4 (Right side): Knit across.
Row 5: Purl across.
Row 6: Knit across.
Rows 7-9: (K3, P3) 10 times.
Row 10: Purl across.
Row 11: Knit across.
Row 12: Purl across.
Repeat Rows 1-12 until square measures approximately 12″ from cast on edge, ending by working a **right** side row.
Bind off all sts leaving last loop on needle.
Edging: Drop loop from needle, insert crochet hook in loop, turn; work 3 sc in each corner and 48 sc evenly spaced across each side *(Fig. 4, page 2)*; join with slip st to first sc, finish off.

7. Cable Check

Additional materials: Cable needle

Cast on 54 sts.
Rows 1-3: Beginning with a **knit** row, work in Stockinette Stitch.
Row 4: Purl across increasing 6 sts evenly spaced across: 60 sts.
Rows 5 (Right side): K3, P6, (K6, P6) 4 times, K3.
Row 6: P3, K6, (P6, K6) 4 times, P3.
Rows 7 and 8: Repeat Rows 5 and 6.
Row 9: K3, P6, ★ work Cable as follows: slip 3 sts onto cable needle and hold in **back** of work, K3, K3 from cable needle **(Cable made)**, P6; repeat from ★ 3 times **more**, K3.
Rows 10-12: Repeat Rows 6-8.
Row 13: K9, P6, (K6, P6) 3 times, K9.
Row 14: P9, K6, (P6, K6) 3 times, P9.
Rows 15 and 16: Repeat Rows 13 and 14.
Row 17: K3, work Cable, (P6, work Cable) 4 times, K3.
Rows 18-20: Repeat Rows 14-16.
Repeat Rows 5-20 until square measures approximately 11¼″ from cast on edge, ending by working Row 12 or Row 20.
Next Row: Knit across decreasing 6 sts evenly spaced: 54 sts.
Last 3 Rows: Beginning with a **purl** row, work in Stockinette Stitch.
Bind off all sts leaving last loop on needle.
Edging: Drop loop from needle, insert crochet hook in loop, do **not** turn; work 3 sc in each corner and 48 sc evenly spaced across each side *(Fig. 4, page 2)*; join with slip st to first sc, finish off.

8. Candle Tree

Additional materials: Cable needle

Back Knit Cross (abbreviated BKC): Slip 1 st onto cable needle and hold in **back** of work, K1, K1 from cable needle.
Front Knit Cross (abbreviated FKC): Slip 1 st onto cable needle and hold in **front** of work, K1, K1 from cable needle.
Front Purl Cross (abbreviated FPC): Slip 1 st onto cable needle and hold in **front** of work, P1, K1 from cable needle.
Back Purl Cross (abbreviated BPC): Slip 1 st onto cable needle and hold in **back** of work, K1, P1 from cable needle.

Cast on 55 sts.
Rows 1-10: Beginning with a **purl** row, work in Reverse Stockinette Stitch.
Row 11 (Right side): P 26, K3, P 26.
Row 12: K 26, P3, K 26.
Rows 13-18: Repeat Rows 11 and 12, 3 times.
Row 19: P 25, BKC, K1, FKC, P 25.
Row 20: K 24, FPC, P3, BPC, K 24.
Row 21: P 23, BPC, P1, K3, P1, FPC, P 23.
Row 22: K 22, FPC, K2, P3, K2, BPC, K 22.
Row 23: P 21, BKC, P3, K3, P3, FKC, P 21.
Row 24: K 20, FPC, P1, K3, P3, K3, P1, BPC, K 20.
Row 25: P 19, BPC, P1, K1, P3, K3, P3, K1, P1, FPC, P 19.
Row 26: K 18, FPC, K2, P1, K3, P3, K3, P1, K2, BPC, K 18.
Row 27: P 17, BKC, P3, YO (**Fig. 1b, page 1**), K1, YO (**Fig. 1c, page 1**), P3, K3, P3, YO, K1, YO, P3, FKC, P 17: 59 sts.
Row 28: K 16, FPC, P1, K3, (P3, K3) 3 times, P1, BPC, K 16.
Row 29: P 15, BPC, P1, K1, P3, K1, [YO (**Fig. 1a, page 1**), K1] twice, P3, K3, P3, K1, (YO, K1) twice, P3, K1, P1, FPC, P 15: 63 sts.
Row 30: K 14, FPC, K2, P1, K3, P5, K3, P3, K3, P5, K3, P1, K2, BPC, K 14.
Row 31: P 13, BPC, P3, K1, P3, K2, YO, K1, YO, K2, P3, K3, P3, K2, YO, K1, YO, K2, P3, K1, P3, FPC, P 13: 67 sts.
Row 32: K 13, P1, K4, P1, K3, P7, K3, P3, K3, P7, K3, P1, K4, P1, K 13.
Row 33: P 13, YO, K1, YO, P4, K1, P3, SSK (**Figs. 3a-c, page 2**), K3, K2 tog, P3, K3, P3, SSK, K3, K2 tog, P3, K1, P4, YO, K1, YO, P 13.
Row 34: K 13, P3, K4, P1, K3, P5, K3, P3, K3, P5, K3, P1, K4, P3, K 13.
Row 35: P 13, K1, (YO, K1) twice, P4, K1, P3, SSK, K1, K2 tog, P3, K3, P3, SSK, K1, K2 tog, P3, K1, P4, K1, (YO, K1) twice, P 13.
Row 36: K 13, P5, K4, P1, K3, (P3, K3) 3 times, P1, K4, P5, K 13.
Note: When instructed to slip a stitch, always slip as if to **knit**.
Row 37: P 13, K2, YO, K1, YO, K2, P4, YO, K1, YO, P3, slip 1, K2 tog, PSSO, P2, BPC, K1, FPC, P2, slip 1, K2 tog, PSSO, P3, YO, K1, YO, P4, K2, YO, K1, YO, K2, P 13: 71 sts.
Row 38: K 13, P7, K4, P3, K3, P1, K2, P1, (K1, P1) twice, K2, P1, K3, P3, K4, P7, K 13.
Row 39: P 13, SSK, K3, K2 tog, P4, K1, (YO, K1) twice, P5, BPC, P1, K1, P1, FPC, P5, K1, (YO, K1) twice, P4, SSK, K3, K2 tog, P 13.
Row 40: K 13, P5, K4, P5, K5, P1, (K2, P1) twice, K5, P5, K4, P5, K 13.
Row 41: P 13, SSK, K1, K2 tog, P4, K2, YO, K1, YO, K2, P4, BPC, P2, K1, P2, FPC, P4, K2, YO, K1, YO, K2, P4, SSK, K1, K2 tog, P 13.

Row 42: K 13, P3, K4, P7, K4, P1, (K3, P1) twice, K4, P7, K4, P3, K 13.
Row 43: P 13, slip 1, K2 tog, PSSO, P4, SSK, K3, K2 tog, P3, BPC, P3, K1, P3, FPC, P3, SSK, K3, K2 tog, P4, slip 1, K2 tog, PSSO, P 13: 63 sts.
Row 44: K 13, P1, K4, P5, K3, P1, (K4, P1) twice, K3, P5, K4, P1, K 13.
Row 45: P 18, SSK, K1, K2 tog, P3, YO, K1, YO, P4, K1, P4, YO, K1, YO, P3, SSK, K1, K2 tog, P 18.
Row 46: K 18, P3, K3, P3, K4, P1, K4, P3, K3, P3, K 18.
Row 47: P 18, slip 1, K2 tog, PSSO, P3, K1, (YO, K1) twice, (P4, K1) twice, (YO, K1) twice, P3, slip 1, K2 tog, PSSO, P 18.
Row 48: K 18, P1, K3, P5, K4, P1, K4, P5, K3, P1, K 18.
Row 49: P 22, K2, YO, K1, YO, K2, P4, YO, K1, YO, P4, K2, YO, K1, YO, K2, P 22.
Row 50: K 22, P7, K4, P3, K4, P7, K 22.
Row 51: P 22, SSK, K3, K2 tog, P4, K1, (YO, K1) twice, P4, SSK, K3, K2 tog, P 22: 67 sts.
Row 52: K 22, P5, (K4, P5) twice, K 22.
Row 53: P 22, SSK, K1, K2 tog, P4, K2, YO, K1, YO, K2, P4, SSK, K1, K2 tog, P 22: 65 sts.
Row 54: K 22, P3, K4, P7, K4, P3, K 22.
Row 55: P 22, slip 1, K2 tog, PSSO, P4, SSK, K3, K2 tog, P4, slip 1, K2 tog, PSSO, P 22: 59 sts.
Row 56: K 22, P1, K4, P5, K4, P1, K 22.
Row 57: P 27, SSK, K1, K2 tog, P 27: 57 sts.
Row 58: K 27, P3, K 27.
Row 59: P 27, slip 1, K2 tog, PSSO, P 27: 55 sts.
Row 60: K 27, P1, K 27.
Work in Reverse Stockinette Stitch until square measures approximately 12″ from cast on edge, ending by working a **knit** row.
Bind off all sts leaving last loop on needle.
Edging: Drop loop from needle, insert crochet hook in loop, do **not** turn; work 3 sc in each corner and 48 sc evenly spaced across each side (**Fig. 4, page 2**); join with slip st to first sc, finish off.

---

9. Trinity Stitch

Cast on 54 sts.
Rows 1-8: Knit across.
Note: When instructed to slip a stitch, always slip as if to **purl**, with yarn held in front (on the wrong side).
Row 9: K5, slip 1, K1, ★ (K, P, K) **all** in next st, P3 tog; repeat from ★ across to last 7 sts, K1, slip 1, K5.
Row 10 (Right side): K7, P 40, K7.
Row 11: K5, slip 1, K1, ★ P3 tog, (K, P, K) **all** in next st; repeat from ★ across to last 7 sts, K1, slip 1, K5.
Row 12: K7, P 40, K7.
Rows 13-71: Repeat Rows 9-12, 14 times; then repeat Rows 9-11, once **more**.
Rows 72-79: Knit across.
Bind off all sts leaving last loop on needle.
Edging: Drop loop from needle, insert crochet hook in loop, do **not** turn; work 3 sc in each corner and 48 sc evenly spaced across each side (**Fig. 4, page 2**); join with slip st to first sc, finish off.

10. Alternating Lace

Cast on 55 sts.
Rows 1-4: Beginning with a **knit** row, work in Stockinette Stitch.
Note: When instructed to slip a stitch, always slip as if to **knit**.
Row 5 (Right side): K5, YO *(Fig. 1a, page 1)*, slip 1, K2 tog, PSSO, YO, (K3, YO, slip 1, K2 tog, PSSO, YO) 7 times, K5.
Row 6: Purl across.
Rows 7-12: Repeat Rows 5 and 6, 3 times.
Row 13: K8, YO, slip 1, K2 tog, PSSO, YO, (K3, YO, slip 1, K2 tog, PSSO, YO) 6 times, K8.
Row 14: Purl across.
Rows 15-20: Repeat Rows 13 and 14, 3 times.
Row 21: K 11, YO, slip 1, K2 tog, PSSO, YO, (K3, YO, slip 1, K2 tog, PSSO, YO) 5 times, K 11.
Row 22: Purl across.
Rows 23-28: Repeat Rows 21 and 22, 3 times.
Row 29: K 14, YO, slip 1, K2 tog, PSSO, YO, (K3, YO, slip 1, K2 tog, PSSO, YO) 4 times, K 14.
Row 30: Purl across.
Rows 31-36: Repeat Rows 29 and 30, 3 times.
Row 37: K 17, YO, slip 1, K2 tog, PSSO, YO, (K3, YO, slip 1, K2 tog, PSSO, YO) 3 times, K 17.
Row 38: Purl across.
Rows 39-44: Repeat Rows 37 and 38, 3 times.
Row 45: K 20, YO, slip 1, K2 tog, PSSO, YO, (K3, YO, slip 1, K2 tog, PSSO, YO) twice, K 20.
Row 46: Purl across.
Rows 47-52: Repeat Rows 45 and 46, 3 times.
Row 53: K 23, YO, slip 1, K2 tog, PSSO, YO, K3, YO, slip 1, K2 tog, PSSO, YO, K 23.
Row 54: Purl across.
Rows 55-60: Repeat Rows 53 and 54, 3 times.
Row 61: K 26, YO, slip 1, K2 tog, PSSO, YO, K 26.
Row 62: Purl across.
Rows 63-68: Repeat Rows 61 and 62, 3 times.
Work in Stockinette Stitch until square measures approximately 12" from cast on edge, ending by working a **knit** row.
Bind off all sts leaving last loop on needle.

Edging: Drop loop from needle, insert crochet hook in loop, turn; work 3 sc in each corner and 48 sc evenly spaced across each side *(Fig. 4, page 2)*; join with slip st to first sc, finish off.

11. Little Shell Pattern

Cast on 55 sts.
Row 1 (Right side): Knit across.
Row 2: Purl across.
Row 3: K4, YO *(Fig. 1c, page 1)*, P1, P3 tog, P1, YO *(Fig. 1b, page 1)*, ★ K2, YO, P1, P3 tog, P1, YO; repeat from ★ across to last 4 sts, K4.
Row 4: Purl across.
Repeat Rows 1-4 until square measures approximately 12" from cast on edge, ending by working a **right** side row.
Bind off all sts leaving last loop on needle.

Edging: Drop loop from needle, insert crochet hook in loop, turn; work 3 sc in each corner and 48 sc evenly spaced across each side *(Fig. 4, page 2)*; join with slip st to first sc, finish off.

12. Lace Loops

Cast on 55 sts.
Rows 1-8: Knit across.
Note: When instructed to slip a stitch, always slip as if to **knit**.
Row 9: (Right side): K 19, YO *(Fig. 1a, page 1)*, slip 1, K1, PSSO, K1, K2 tog, YO, K1, YO, slip 1, K1, PSSO, K 28.
Row 10 AND ALL WRONG SIDE ROWS: K5, purl across to last 5 sts, K5.
Row 11: K 20, YO, slip 1, K2 tog, PSSO, YO, K3, YO, slip 1, K1, PSSO, K3, K2 tog, YO, K 22.
Row 13: K 21, YO, slip 1, K1, PSSO, K4, YO, slip 1, K1, PSSO, K1, K2 tog, YO, K1, YO, slip 1, K1, PSSO, K 20.
Row 15: K 28, YO, K3 tog, YO, K3, YO, slip 1, K1, PSSO, K 19.
Row 17: K 28, K2 tog, YO, K5, YO, slip 1, K1, PSSO, K 18.
Row 19: K 27, K2 tog, YO, K1, YO, slip 1, K1, PSSO, K1, K2 tog, YO, K 20.
Row 21: K 21, YO, slip 1, K1, PSSO, K3, K2 tog, YO, K3, YO, K3 tog, YO, K 21.
Row 23: K 19, K2 tog, YO, K1, YO, slip 1, K1, PSSO, K1, K2 tog, YO, K4, K2 tog, YO, K 22.
Row 25: K 18, K2 tog, YO, K3, YO, slip 1, K2 tog, PSSO, YO, K 29.
Row 27: K 17, K2 tog, YO, K5, YO, slip 1, K1, PSSO, K 29.
Row 29: K 19, YO, slip 1, K1, PSSO, K1, K2 tog, YO, K1, YO, slip 1, K1, PSSO, K 28.
Rows 30-68: Repeat Rows 10-29 once, then repeat Rows 10-28 once **more**.
Rows 69-76: Knit across.
Bind off all sts leaving last loop on needle.

Edging: Drop loop from needle, insert crochet hook in loop, do **not** turn; work 3 sc in each corner and 48 sc evenly spaced across each side *(Fig. 4, page 2)*; join with slip st to first sc, finish off.

13. Germaine Stitch

Additional materials: Cable needle

Note: When instructed to slip a stitch, always slip as if to **knit**.

Cast on 63 sts.
Row 1 AND ALL WRONG SIDE ROWS: Purl across.
Row 2 (Right side): P1, K6, ★ YO *(Fig. 1a, page 1)*, slip 1, K1, PSSO, K1, K2 tog, YO, K6; repeat from ★ 4 times **more**, P1.
Row 4: P1, K7, YO, slip 1, K2 tog, PSSO, YO, ★ K8, YO, slip 1, K2 tog, PSSO, YO; repeat from ★ 3 times **more**, K7, P1.
Row 6: Repeat Row 2.
Row 8: P1, work Cable as follows: slip 3 sts onto cable needle and hold in **back** of work, K3, K3 from cable needle (Cable made), ★ K1, YO, slip 1, K2 tog, PSSO, YO, K1, work Cable; repeat from ★ 4 times **more**, P1.
Repeat Rows 1-8 until square measures approximately 12" from cast on edge, ending by working a **purl** row.
Bind off all sts leaving last loop on needle.

Edging: Drop loop from needle, insert crochet hook in loop, do **not** turn; work 3 sc in each corner and 48 sc evenly spaced across each side *(Fig. 4, page 2)*; join with slip st to first sc, finish off.

8

14. Willow Bud Tree

Cast on 55 sts.
Row 1: Purl across.
Row 2 (Right side): Knit across.
Rows 3 and 4: Repeat Rows 1 and 2.
Row 5: P 13, K 11, P7, K 11, P 13.
Row 6: K 13, P 12, K5, P 12, K 13.
Row 7: P 13, K 12, P5, K 12, P 13.
Row 8: K 13, P 13, K3, P 13, K 13.
Row 9: P 13, K 13, P3, K 13, P 13.
Rows 10-15: Repeat Rows 8 and 9, 3 times.
Row 16: K 13, P 11, P2 tog, knit into the front **and** into the back of next st **(knit increase made)**, K1, knit increase, P2 tog, P 11, K 13.
Row 17: P 13, K 12, P5, K 12, P 13.
Row 18: K 13, P 10, P2 tog, YO (**Fig. 1b, page 1**), K1, YO (**Fig. 1a, page 1**), K3, YO, K1, YO (**Fig. 1c, page 1**), P2 tog, P 10, K 13: 57 sts.
Row 19: P 13, K 11, P3, purl into the front **and** into the back of next st **(purl increase made)**, P1, purl increase, P3, K 11, P 13: 59 sts.
Row 20: K 13, P9, P2 tog, K1, (YO, K1) twice, (P2, K1) twice, (YO, K1) twice, P2 tog, P9, K 13: 61 sts.
Row 21: P 13, K 10, P5, K1, knit increase, P1, knit increase, K1, P5, K 10, P 13: 63 sts.
Row 22: K 13, P8, P2 tog, K2, YO, K1, YO, K2, P3, K1, P3, K2, YO, K1, YO, K2, P2 tog, P8, K 13: 65 sts.
Row 23: P 13, K9, P7, K1, knit increase, K1, P1, K1, knit increase, K1, P7, K9, P 13: 67 sts.
Row 24: K 13, P7, P2 tog, K3, YO, K1, YO, K3, (P3, K3) twice, YO, K1, YO, K3, P2 tog, P7, K 13: 69 sts.
Row 25: P 13, K8, P9, K1, knit increase, K1, P3, K1, knit increase, K1, P9, K8, P 13: 71 sts.
Row 26: K 13, P6, P2 tog, K4, YO, K1, YO, K4, P4, K3, P4, K4, YO, K1, YO, K4, P2 tog, P6, K 13: 73 sts.
Row 27: P 13, K7, P 11, K1, knit increase, K2, P3, K2, knit increase, K1, P 11, K7, P 13: 75 sts.
Note: When instructed to slip a stitch, always slip as if to **knit**.
Row 28: K 13, P5, P2 tog, slip 1, K1, PSSO, K7, K2 tog, P5, K3, P5, slip 1, K1, PSSO, K7, K2 tog, P2 tog, P5, K 13: 69 sts.
Row 29: P 13, K6, P9, K5, purl increase, P1, purl increase, K5, P9, K6, P 13: 71 sts.
Row 30: K 13, P4, P2 tog, slip 1, K1, PSSO, K5, K2 tog, P5, YO, K1, YO, P1, K1, P1, YO, K1, YO, P5, slip 1, K1, PSSO, K5, K2 tog, P2 tog, P4, K 13: 69 sts.
Row 31: P 13, K5, P7, K5, P3, knit increase, P1, knit increase, P3, K5, P7, K5, P 13: 71 sts.
Row 32: K 13, P3, P2 tog, slip 1, K1, PSSO, K3, K2 tog, P5, K1, (YO, K1) twice, (P2, K1) twice, (YO, K1) twice, P5, slip 1, K1, PSSO, K3, K2 tog, P2 tog, P3, K 13: 69 sts.
Row 33: P 13, K4, P5, K5, P5, K1, knit increase, P1, knit increase, K1, P5, K5, P5, K4, P 13: 71 sts.
Row 34: K 13, P2, P2 tog, slip 1, K1, PSSO, K1, K2 tog, P5, K2, YO, K1, YO, K2, P3, K1, P3, K2, YO, K1, YO, K2, P5, slip 1, K1, PSSO, K1, K2 tog, P2 tog, P2, K 13: 69 sts.
Row 35: P 13, K3, P3, K5, P7, K1, knit increase, P3, knit increase, K1, P7, K5, P3, K3, P 13: 71 sts.
Row 36: K 13, P1, P2 tog, K3 tog, P5, K3, YO, K1, YO, K3, (P3, K3) twice, YO, K1, YO, K3, P5, K3 tog, P2 tog, P1, K 13: 69 sts.
Rows 37-39: Repeat Rows 25-27: 75 sts.
Row 40: K 13, P5, P2 tog, slip 1, K1, PSSO, K7, K2 tog, P6, YO, K1, YO, P6, slip 1, K1, PSSO, K7, K2 tog, P2 tog, P5, K 13: 71 sts.
Row 41: P 13, K6, P9, K6, P3, K6, P9, K6, P 13.
Row 42: K 13, P6, slip 1, K1, PSSO, K5, K2 tog, P6, K1, (YO, K1) twice, P6, slip 1, K1, PSSO, K5, K2 tog, P6, K 13: 69 sts.

Row 43: P 13, K6, P7, K6, P5, K6, P7, K6, P 13.
Row 44: K 13, P6, slip 1, K1, PSSO, K3, K2 tog, P6, K2, YO, K1, YO, K2, P6, slip 1, K1, PSSO, K3, K2 tog, P6, K 13: 67 sts.
Row 45: P 13, K6, P5, K6, P7, K6, P5, K6, P 13.
Row 46: K 13, P6, slip 1, K1, PSSO, K1, K2 tog, P6, K3, YO, K1, YO, K3, P6, slip 1, K1, PSSO, K1, K2 tog, P6, K 13: 65 sts.
Row 47: P 13, K6, P3, K6, P9, K6, P3, K6, P 13.
Row 48: K 13, P6, K3 tog, P6, K4, YO, K1, YO, K4, P6, K3 tog, P6, K 13: 63 sts.
Row 49: P 13, K 13, P 11, K 13, P 13.
Row 50: K 13, P 13, slip 1, K1, PSSO, K7, K2 tog, P 13, K 13: 61 sts.
Row 51: P 13, K 13, P9, K 13, P 13.
Row 52: K 13, P 13, slip 1, K1, PSSO, K5, K2 tog, P 13, K 13: 59 sts.
Row 53: P 13, K 13, P7, K 13, P 13.
Row 54: K 13, P 13, slip 1, K1, PSSO, K3, K2 tog, P 13, K 13: 57 sts.
Row 55: P 13, K 13, P5, K 13, P 13.
Row 56: K 13, P 13, slip 1, K1, PSSO, K1, K2 tog, P 13, K 13: 55 sts.
Row 57: P 13, K 13, P3, K 13, P 13.
Row 58: K 13, P 13, K3 tog, P 13, K 13: 53 sts.
Row 59: P 13, K 12, knit increase, K1, knit increase, K 12, P 13: 55 sts.
Row 60: K 13, P 29, K 13.
Row 61: P 13, K 29, P 13.
Repeat Rows 60 and 61 until square measures approximately 12″ from cast on edge, ending by working Row 60.
Bind off all sts leaving last loop on needle.
Edging: Drop loop from needle, insert crochet hook in loop, turn; work 3 sc in each corner and 48 sc evenly spaced across each side (**Fig. 4, page 2**); join with slip st to first sc, finish off.

---

15. Six-Stitch Cable

Additional materials: Cable needle

Cast on 78 sts.
Row 1 AND ALL WRONG SIDE ROWS: P1, (K2, P6, K2, P1) across.
Row 2 (Right side): K1, (P2, K6, P2, K1) across.
Row 4: K1, (P2, K6, P2, K1) across.
Row 6: K1, ★ P2, slip 3 sts onto cable needle and hold in **back** of work, K3, K3 from cable needle, P2, K1; repeat from ★ across.
Row 8: K1, (P2, K6, P2, K1) across.
Repeat Rows 1-8 until square measures approximately 12″ from cast on edge, ending by working Row 2.
Bind off all sts leaving last loop on needle.
Edging: Drop loop from needle, insert crochet hook in loop, turn; work 3 sc in each corner and 48 sc evenly spaced across each side (**Fig. 4, page 2**); join with slip st to first sc, finish off.

16. Inverness Diamond

Cast on 51 sts.
Row 1: P1, K3, P9, K3, (P2, K3, P9, K3) twice, P1.
Row 2 (Right side): K2, P3, K7, P3, (K4, P3, K7, P3) twice, K2.
Row 3: P3, K3, P5, K3, (P6, K3, P5, K3) twice, P3.
Row 4: K4, P3, K3, P3, (K8, P3, K3, P3) twice, K4.
Row 5: P5, K3, P1, K3, (P 10, K3, P1, K3) twice, P5.
Row 6: K6, P5, (K 12, P5) twice, K6.
Row 7: P7, K3, (P 14, K3) twice, P7.
Row 8: K6, P5, (K 12, P5) twice, K6.
Row 9: P5, K3, P1, K3, (P 10, K3, P1, K3) twice, P5.
Row 10: K4, P3, K3, P3, (K8, P3, K3, P3) twice, K4.
Row 11: P3, K3, P5, K3, (P6, K3, P5, K3) twice, P3.
Row 12: K2, P3, K7, P3, (K4, P3, K7, P3) twice, K2.
Repeat Rows 1-12 until square measures approximately 12″ from cast on edge, ending by working a **right** side row.
Bind off all sts leaving last loop on needle.
Edging: Drop loop from needle, insert crochet hook in loop, turn; work 3 sc in each corner and 48 sc evenly spaced across each side **(Fig. 4, page 2)**; join with slip st to first sc, finish off.

17. Hourglass Eyelets

Note: When instructed to slip a stitch, always slip as if to **knit**.

Cast on 54 sts.
Row 1 (Right side): Knit across.
Row 2: Purl across.
Row 3: Knit across.
Row 4: Purl across increasing 7 sts evenly spaced: 61 sts.
Row 5: K9, P1, (K5, P1) 7 times, K9.
Row 6: P3, K1, (P5, K1) 9 times, P3.
Row 7: K4, YO **(Fig. 1a, page 1)**, slip 1, K1, PSSO, P1, K2 tog, YO, ★ K1, YO, slip 1, K1, PSSO, P1, K2 tog, YO; repeat from ★ across to last 4 sts, K4.
Row 8: P3, K1, P2, K1, (P5, K1) 8 times, P2, K1, P3.
Row 9: K6, P1, (K5, P1) 8 times, K6.
Row 10: P3, K1, P2, K1, (P5, K1) 8 times, P2, K1, P3.
Row 11: K4, K2 tog, YO, K1, YO, slip 1, K1, PSSO, ★ P1, K2 tog, YO, K1, YO, slip 1, K1, PSSO; repeat from ★ across to last 4 sts, K4.
Row 12: P3, K1, (P5, K1) 9 times, P3.
Repeat Rows 5-12 until square measures approximately 11¼″ from cast on edge, ending by working a **wrong** side row.
Next Row: Knit across decreasing 7 sts evenly spaced: 54 sts.
Last 3 Rows: Repeat Rows 2 and 3 once, then repeat Row 2 once **more**.
Bind off all sts leaving last loop on needle.
Edging: Drop loop from needle, insert crochet hook in loop, do **not** turn; work 3 sc in each corner and 48 sc evenly spaced across each side **(Fig. 4, page 2)**; join with slip st to first sc, finish off.

18. Moss Panels

Cast on 55 sts.
Row 1 (Right side): Purl across.
Row 2: K3, (P1, K3) across.
Row 3: P3, (K1, P3) across.
Row 4: K2, P1, K1, P1, K2, (P1, K2, P1, K1, P1, K2) 6 times.
Row 5: P2, K1, P1, K1, P2, (K1, P2, K1, P1, K1, P2) 6 times.
Row 6: K1, (P1, K1) across.
Row 7: P1, (K1, P1) across.
Rows 8 and 9: Repeat Rows 4 and 5.
Rows 10 and 11: Repeat Rows 2 and 3.
Repeat Rows 2-11 until square measures approximately 12″ from cast on edge, ending by working a **right** side row.
Bind off all sts leaving last loop on needle.
Edging: Drop loop from needle, insert crochet hook in loop, turn; work 3 sc in each corner and 48 sc evenly spaced across each side **(Fig. 4, page 2)**; join with slip st to first sc, finish off.

19. Twisted Cable

Additional materials: Cable needle

Cast on 73 sts.
Row 1 AND ALL WRONG SIDE ROWS: P1, (K1, P5, K1, P1) across.
Row 2 (Right side): K1, ★ P1, slip 4 sts onto cable needle and hold in **back** of work, K1, slip last 3 sts from cable needle back onto left needle and knit them, K1 from cable needle, P1, K1; repeat from ★ across.
Row 4: K1, (P1, K5, P1, K1) across.
Row 6: K1, (P1, K5, P1, K1) across.
Repeat Rows 1-6 until square measures approximately 12″ from cast on edge, ending by working a **wrong** side row.
Bind off all sts leaving last loop on needle.
Edging: Drop loop from needle, insert crochet hook in loop, do **not** turn; work 3 sc in each corner and 48 sc evenly spaced across each side **(Fig. 4, page 2)**; join with slip st to first sc, finish off.

20. Large Bobble Rib

Note: Work Bobble as follows: (K, K tbl, K) **all** in next st, **turn**, K3, **turn**, P3, **turn**, K3, **turn**, slip 1 as if to **knit**, K2 tog, PSSO.

Cast on 65 sts.
Row 1 (Right side): K2, (P2, K1, P2, K2) across.
Row 2: P2, (K2, P1, K2, P2) across.
Row 3: K2, (P2, work Bobble, P2, K2) across.
Row 4: P2, (K2, P1, K2, P2) across.
Repeat Rows 1-4 until square measures approximately 12″ from cast on edge, ending by working Row 1.
Bind off all sts leaving last loop on needle.
Edging: Drop loop from needle, insert crochet hook in loop, turn; work 3 sc in each corner and 48 sc evenly spaced across each side **(Fig. 4, page 2)**; join with slip st to first sc, finish off.

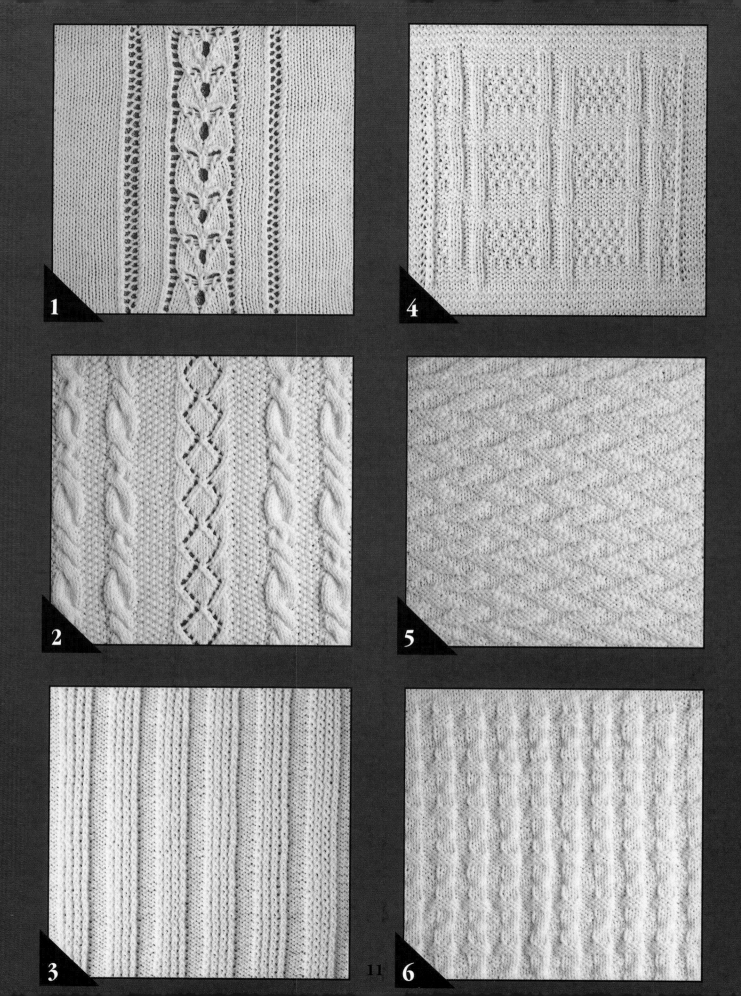

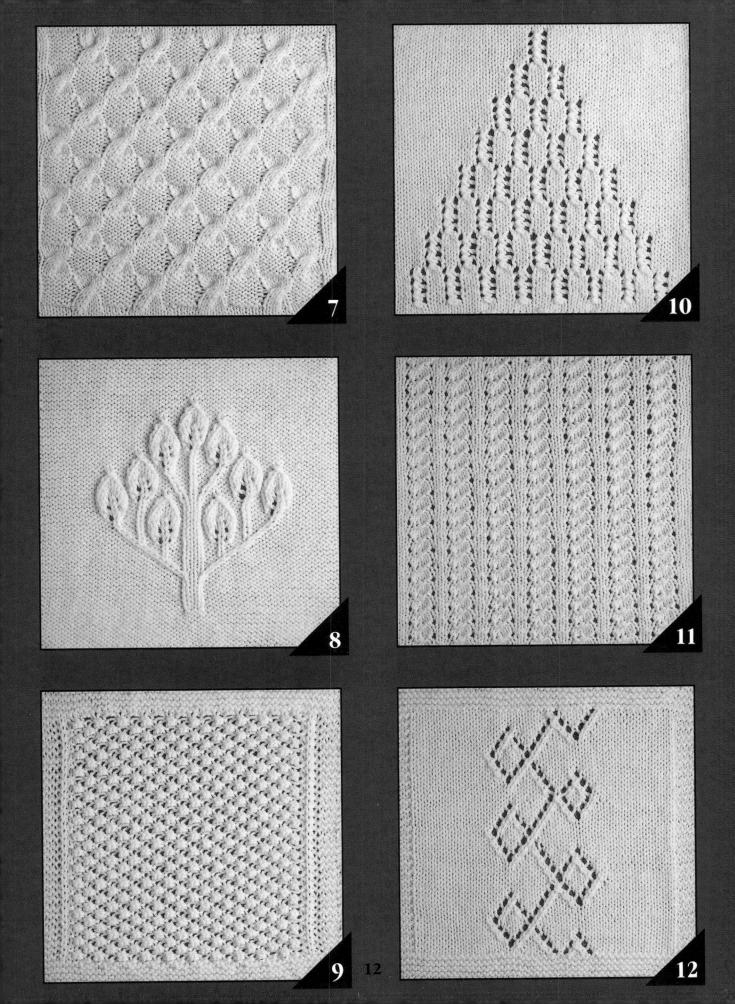

13

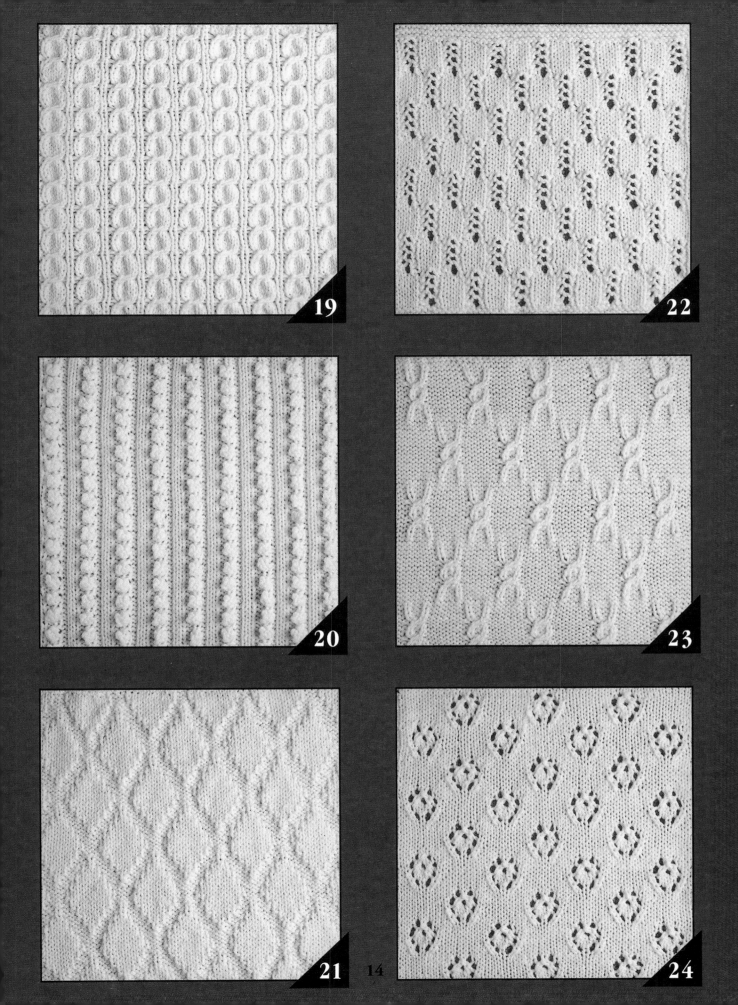

19

22

20

23

21

14

24

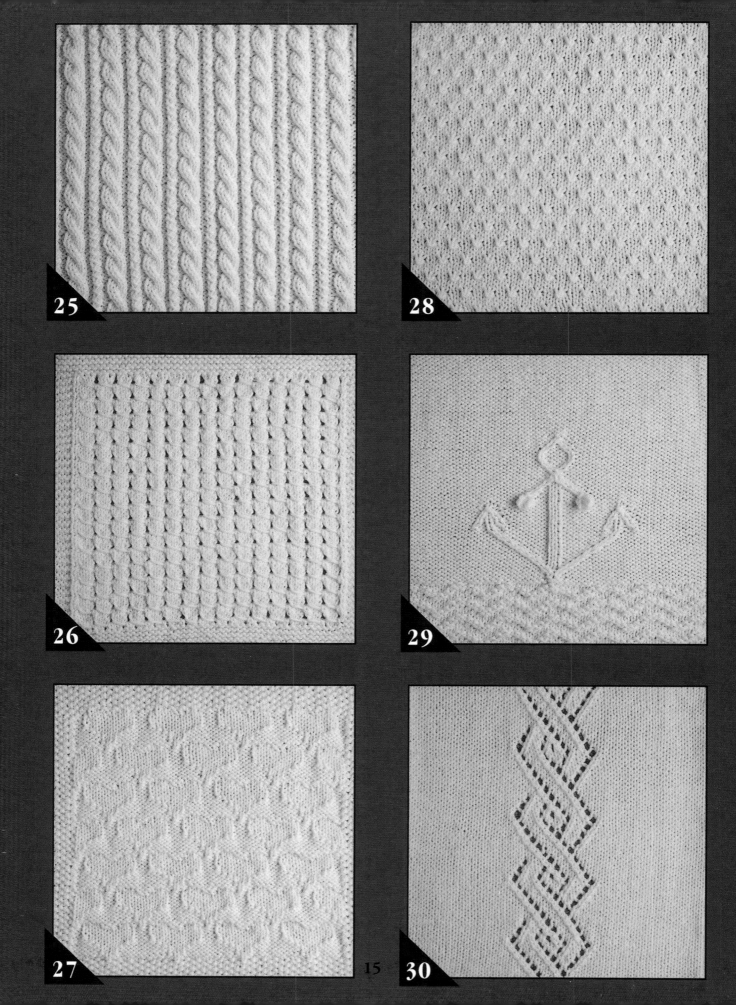

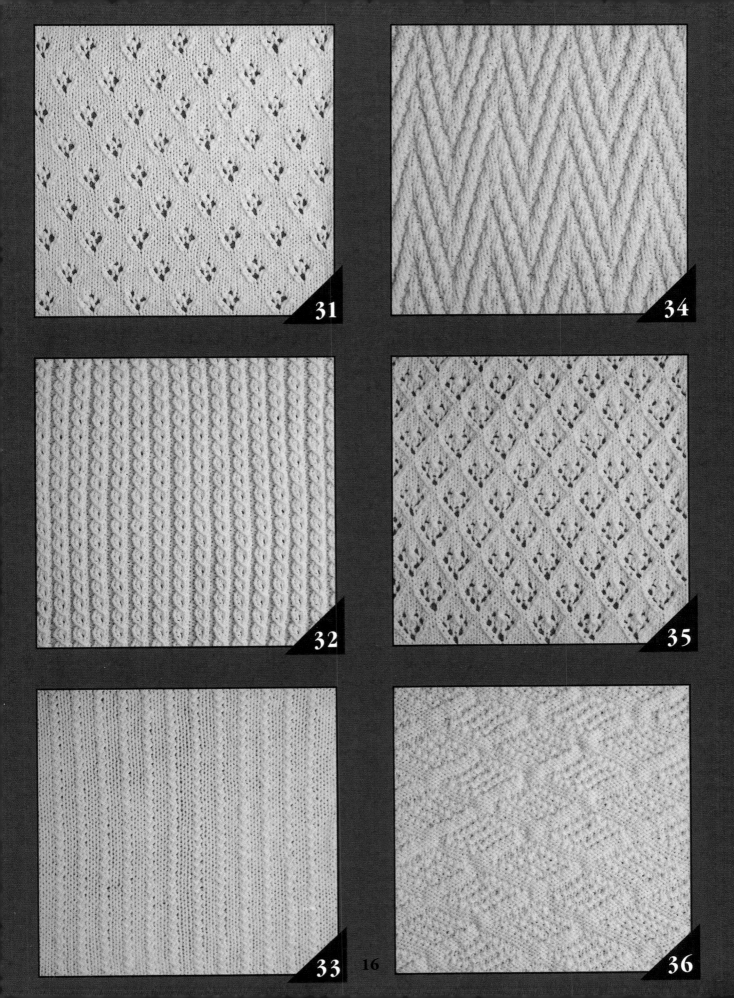

17

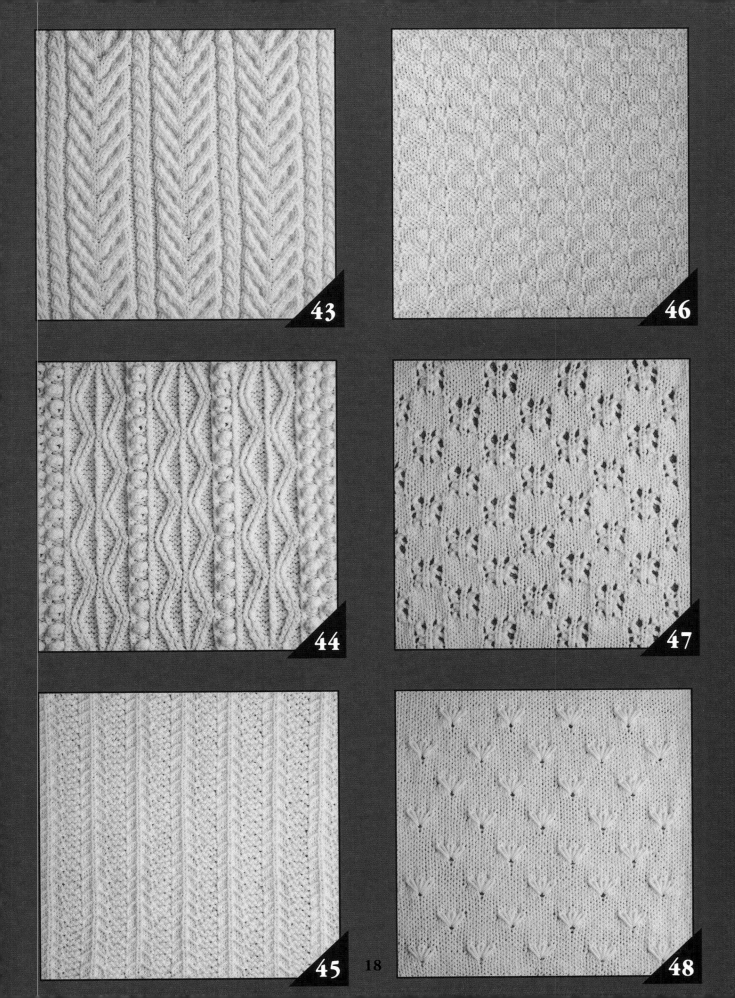

43

46

44

47

45

18

48

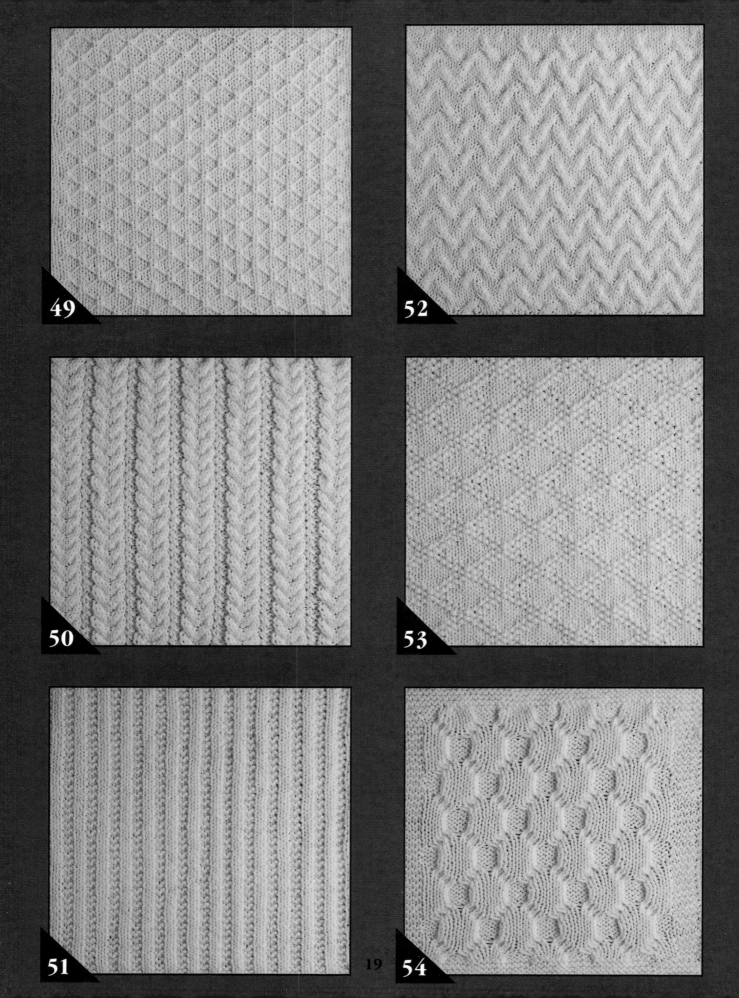

49

52

50

53

51

19

54

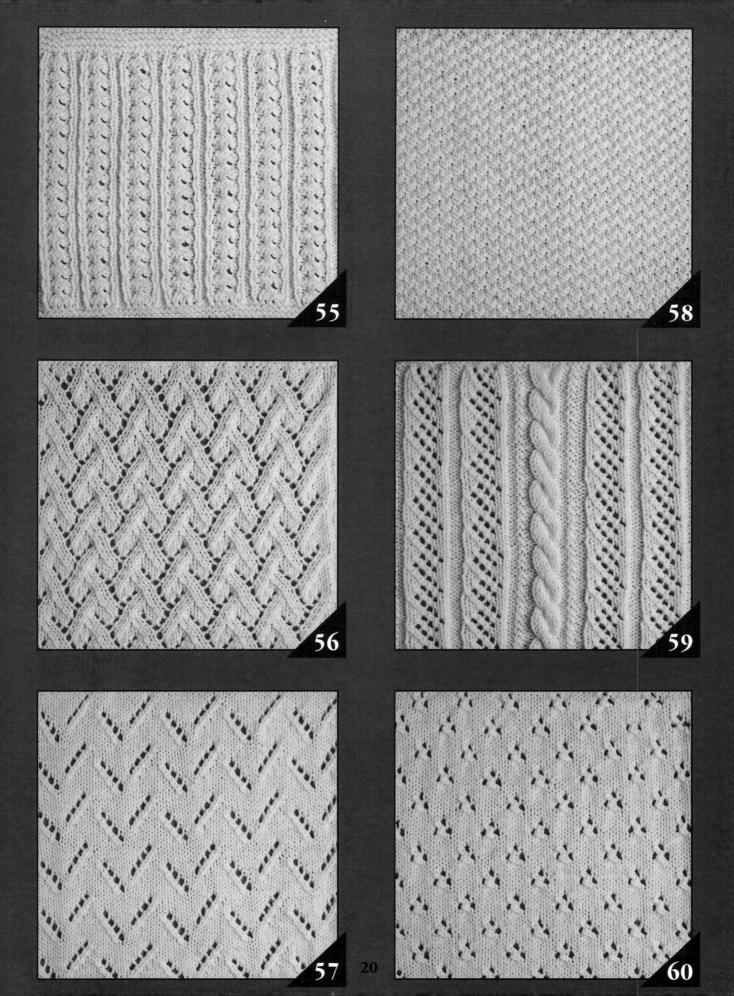

55

58

56

59

57

60

21. Imitation Lattice

Cast on 61 sts.
Row 1 (Right side): K4, P5, (K7, P5) 4 times, K4.
Row 2: P4, K5, (P7, K5) 4 times, P4.
Row 3: K3, P3, K1, P3, (K5, P3, K1, P3) 4 times, K3.
Row 4: P3, K3, P1, K3, (P5, K3, P1, K3) 4 times, P3.
Row 5: K2, P3, (K3, P3) 9 times, K2.
Row 6: P2, K3, (P3, K3) 9 times, P2.
Row 7: K1, (P3, K5, P3, K1) 5 times.
Row 8: P1, (K3, P5, K3, P1) 5 times.
Row 9: P3, K7, (P5, K7) 4 times, P3.
Row 10: K3, P7, (K5, P7) 4 times, K3.
Row 11: P2, K9, (P3, K9) 4 times, P2.
Row 12: K2, P9, (K3, P9) 4 times, K2.
Rows 13 and 14: Repeat Rows 9 and 10.
Rows 15 and 16: Repeat Rows 7 and 8.
Rows 17 and 18: Repeat Rows 5 and 6.
Rows 19 and 20: Repeat Rows 3 and 4.
Rows 21 and 22: Repeat Rows 1 and 2.
Row 23: K5, P3, (K9, P3) 4 times, K5.
Row 24: P5, K3, (P9, K3) 4 times, P5.
Repeat Rows 1-24 until square measures approximately 12″ from cast on edge, ending by working a **right** side row.
Bind off all sts leaving last loop on needle.
Edging: Drop loop from needle, insert crochet hook in loop, turn; work 3 sc in each corner and 48 sc evenly spaced across each side (*Fig. 4, page 2*); join with slip st to first sc, finish off.

---

22. Wheatear Stitch

Cast on 56 sts.
Rows 1-7: Knit across.
Note: When instructed to slip a stitch, always slip as if to **knit**.
Row 8: P6, K2, YO (*Fig. 1a, page 1*), slip 1, K1, PSSO, ★ P4, K2, YO, slip 1, K1, PSSO; repeat from ★ across to last 6 sts, P6.
Row 9 (Right side): K6, P2, YO (*Fig. 1d, page 1*), P2 tog, ★ K4, P2, YO, P2 tog; repeat from ★ across to last 6 sts, K6.
Rows 10-15: Repeat Rows 8 and 9, 3 times.
Row 16: P2, K2, YO, slip 1, K1, PSSO, ★ P4, K2, YO, slip 1, K1, PSSO; repeat from ★ across to last 2 sts, P2.
Row 17: K2, P2, YO, P2 tog, ★ K4, P2, YO, P2 tog; repeat from ★ across to last 2 sts, K2.
Rows 18-23: Repeat Rows 16 and 17, 3 times.
Rows 24-71: Repeat Rows 8-23, 3 times.
Rows 72-77: Knit across.
Bind off all sts leaving last loop on needle.
Edging: Drop loop from needle, insert crochet hook in loop, turn; work 3 sc in each corner and 48 sc evenly spaced across each side (*Fig. 4, page 2*); join with slip st to first sc, finish off.

---

23. Little Bow Twist

Additional materials: Cable needle

Cast on 61 sts.
Row 1 (Right side): Purl across.
Row 2: Knit across.
Row 3: P4, K1, P3, K1, (P7, K1, P3, K1) 4 times, P4.
Row 4: K4, P1, K3, P1, (K7, P1, K3, P1) 4 times, K4.
Rows 5 and 6: Repeat Rows 3 and 4.
Row 7: P4, work Twist as follows: slip 4 sts onto cable needle and hold in **back** of work, K1, slip 3 **purl** sts from cable needle back onto left needle and purl them, K1 from cable needle (**Twist made**), (P7, work Twist) 4 times, P4.
Rows 8-14: Repeat Rows 4-7 once, then repeat Rows 4-6 once **more**.
Row 15: Purl across.
Row 16: Knit across.
Row 17: P 10, K1, P3, K1, (P7, K1, P3, K1) 3 times, P 10.
Row 18: K 10, P1, K3, P1, (K7, P1, K3, P1) 3 times, K 10.
Rows 19 and 20: Repeat Rows 17 and 18.
Row 21: P 10, work Twist, (P7, work Twist) 3 times, P 10.
Rows 22-28: Repeat Rows 18-21 once, then repeat Rows 18-20 once **more**.
Rows 29 and 30: Repeat Rows 15 and 16.
Repeat Rows 3-30 until square measures approximately 12″ from cast on edge, ending by working Row 16.
Bind off all sts leaving last loop on needle.
Edging: Drop loop from needle, insert crochet hook in loop, do **not** turn; work 3 sc in each corner and 48 sc evenly spaced across each side (*Fig. 4, page 2*); join with slip st to first sc, finish off.

---

24. Rosebud Pattern

Note: When instructed to slip a stitch, always slip as if to **knit**.

Cast on 53 sts.
Row 1 AND ALL WRONG SIDE ROWS: Purl across.
Row 2 (Right side): K 10, K2 tog, YO (*Fig. 1a, page 1*), K1, YO, SSK (*Figs. 3a-c, page 2*), (K9, K2 tog, YO, K1, YO, SSK) twice, K 10.
Row 4: K9, K2 tog, YO, K3, YO, SSK, (K7, K2 tog, YO, K3, YO, SSK) twice, K9.
Row 6: K 10, YO, SSK, YO, K3 tog, YO, (K9, YO, SSK, YO, K3 tog, YO) twice, K 10.
Row 8: K 11, (YO, slip 1, K2 tog, PSSO, YO, K 11) across.
Row 10: K3, K2 tog, YO, K1, YO, SSK, (K9, K2 tog, YO, K1, YO, SSK) 3 times, K3.
Row 12: K2, K2 tog, YO, K3, YO, SSK, (K7, K2 tog, YO, K3, YO, SSK) 3 times, K2.
Row 14: K3, YO, SSK, YO, K3 tog, YO, (K9, YO, SSK, YO, K3 tog, YO) 3 times, K3.
Row 16: K4, YO, slip 1, K2 tog, PSSO, YO, (K 11, YO, slip 1, K2 tog, PSSO, YO) 3 times, K4.
Repeat Rows 1-16 until square measures approximately 12″ from cast on edge, ending by working a **purl** row.
Bind off all sts leaving last loop on needle.
Edging: Drop loop from needle, insert crochet hook in loop, do **not** turn; work 3 sc in each corner and 48 sc evenly spaced across each side (*Fig. 4, page 2*); join with slip st to first sc, finish off.

25. Cable Panels

Additional materials: Cable needle

Cable: Slip 2 sts onto cable needle and hold in **front** of work, K2, K2 from cable needle.
Twist: With yarn in back, insert right needle through next st as if to **purl**, knit second st on needle and draw loop through first st **(Fig. 9a)**, then knit into the **back** of first st **(Fig. 9b)** letting both sts drop off needle together.

Fig. 9a   **Fig. 9b**

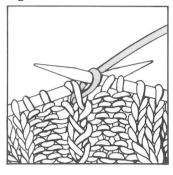   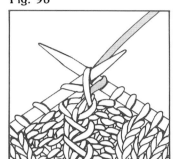

Cast on 84 sts.
Row 1 AND ALL WRONG SIDE ROWS: K1, P2, (K2, P4, K2, P2) 8 times, K1.
Row 2 (Right side): P1, work Twist, (P2, work Cable, P2, work Twist) 8 times, P1.
Row 4: P1, work Twist, (P2, K4, P2, work Twist) 8 times, P1.
Row 6: P1, work Twist, (P2, K4, P2, work Twist) 8 times, P1.
Repeat Rows 1-6 until square measures approximately 12″ from cast on edge, ending by working a **wrong** side row.
Bind off all sts leaving last loop on needle.
Edging: Drop loop from needle, insert crochet hook in loop, do **not** turn; work 3 sc in each corner and 48 sc evenly spaced across each side **(Fig. 4, page 2)**; join with slip st to first sc, finish off.

---

26. Mrs. Hunter's Pattern

Cast on 54 sts.
Rows 1-7: Knit across.
Row 8: Knit across increasing 18 sts evenly spaced: 72 sts.
Row 9: K5, purl across to last 5 sts, K5.
Row 10 (Right side): K6, (slip 1 as if to **purl**, K3, PSSO) across to last 6 sts, K6: 57 sts.
Row 11: K5, P4, YO **(Fig. 1d, page 1)**, (P3, YO) across to last 6 sts, P1, K5: 72 sts.
Row 12: Knit across.
Repeat Rows 9-12 until square measures approximately 11″ from cast on edge, ending by working Row 9.
Next Row: Knit across decreasing 18 sts evenly spaced.
Last 7 Rows: Knit across.
Bind off all sts leaving last loop on needle.
Edging: Drop loop from needle, insert crochet hook in loop, do **not** turn; work 3 sc in each corner and 48 sc evenly spaced across each side **(Fig. 4, page 2)**; join with slip st to first sc, finish off.

27. Valentine Hearts

Cast on 59 sts.
Rows 1-8: K1, (P1, K1) across.
Row 9 (Right side): K1, (P1, K1) twice, P6, K1, (P 11, K1) 3 times, P6, K1, (P1, K1) twice.
Row 10: (K1, P1) twice, K6, P3, (K9, P3) 3 times, K6, (P1, K1) twice.
Row 11: K1, (P1, K1) twice, P5, K3, (P9, K3) 3 times, P5, K1, (P1, K1) twice.
Row 12: (K1, P1) twice, K5, P5, (K7, P5) 3 times, K5, (P1, K1) twice.
Row 13: K1, (P1, K1) twice, P3, K7, (P5, K7) 3 times, P3, K1, (P1, K1) twice.
Row 14: (K1, P1) twice, K3, (P9, K3) 4 times, (P1, K1) twice.
Row 15: K1, (P1, K1) twice, P2, K9, (P3, K9) 3 times, P2, K1, (P1, K1) twice.
Row 16: Repeat Row 14.
Row 17: K1, (P1, K1) twice, P2, K4, P1, K4, (P3, K4, P1, K4) 3 times, P2, K1, (P1, K1) twice.
Row 18: K1, (P1, K1) twice, (P1, K2, P2, K3, P2, K2) 4 times, (P1, K1) 3 times.
Row 19: (K1, P1) twice, K2, P 11, (K1, P 11) 3 times, K2, (P1, K1) twice.
Row 20: Repeat Row 15.
Row 21: Repeat Row 14.
Row 22: Repeat Row 13.
Row 23: Repeat Row 12.
Row 24: Repeat Row 11.
Rows 25 and 26: Repeat Rows 10 and 11.
Row 27: K1, (P1, K1) twice, (P1, K4, P3, K4) 4 times, (P1, K1) 3 times.
Row 28: (K1, P1) twice, K3, (P2, K2, P1, K2, P2, K3) 4 times, (P1, K1) twice.
Rows 29-78: Repeat Rows 9-28 twice, then repeat Rows 9-18 once **more**.
Rows 79-86: K1, (P1, K1) across.
Bind off all sts leaving last loop on needle.
Edging: Drop loop from needle, insert crochet hook in loop, do **not** turn; work 3 sc in each corner and 48 sc evenly spaced across each side **(Fig. 4, page 2)**; join with slip st to first sc, finish off.

---

28. Elm Seeds

Cast on 54 sts.
Row 1 (Right side): Knit across.
Row 2: P1, YO **(Fig. 1d, page 1)**, P2, pass YO over the P2, ★ P2, YO, P2, pass YO over the P2; repeat from ★ across to last 3 sts, P3.
Row 3: Knit across.
Row 4: Purl across.
Row 5: Knit across.
Row 6: P3, YO, P2, pass YO over the P2, ★ P2, YO, P2, pass YO over the P2; repeat from ★ across to last st, P1.
Row 7: Knit across.
Row 8: Purl across.
Repeat Rows 1-8 until square measures approximately 12″ from cast on edge, ending by working a **knit** row.
Bind off all sts leaving last loop on needle.
Edging: Drop loop from needle, insert crochet hook in loop, turn; work 3 sc in each corner and 48 sc evenly spaced across each side **(Fig. 4, page 2)**; join with slip st to first sc, finish off.

29. The Anchor

Additional Materials: Cable needle

Back Knit Cross (abbreviated BKC): Slip 1 st onto cable needle and hold in **back** of work, K1, K1 from cable needle.
Front Knit Cross (abbreviated FKC): Slip 1 st onto cable needle and hold in **front** of work, K1, K1 from cable needle.
Front Purl Cross (abbreviated FPC): Slip 1 st onto cable needle and hold in **front** of work, P1, K1 from cable needle.
Back Purl Cross (abbreviated BPC): Slip 1 st onto cable needle and hold in **back** of work, K1, P1 from cable needle.
Bobble: [K1, (YO, K1) twice] **all** in next st, **turn**, P5, **turn**, K5, **turn**, P2 tog, P1, P2 tog, **turn**, slip 1 as if to **knit**, K2 tog, PSSO.

Cast on 54 sts.
Row 1 (Right side): K6, (P2, K6) across.
Row 2: K1, P4, (K4, P4) 6 times, K1.
Row 3: P2, (K2, P2) across.
Row 4: P1, K4, (P4, K4) 6 times, P1.
Row 5: K2, P2, (K6, P2) 6 times, K2.
Row 6: P6, (K2, P6) across.
Row 7: P1, K4, (P4, K4) 6 times, P1.
Row 8: K2, (P2, K2) across.
Row 9: K1, P4, (K4, P4) 6 times, K1.
Row 10: P2, K2, (P6, K2) 6 times, P2.
Rows 11-20: Repeat Rows 1-10.
Row 21: Purl across.
Row 22: Knit across.
Row 23: P 26, K2, P 26.
Row 24: K 26, P2, K 26.
Row 25: P 25, BKC, FKC, P 25.
Row 26: K 24, FPC, P2, BPC, K 24.
Row 27: P 23, BPC, P1, K2, P1, FPC, P 23.
Row 28: K 22, FPC, K2, P2, K2, BPC, K 22.
Row 29: P 21, BPC, P3, K2, P3, FPC, P 21.
Row 30: K 20, FPC, K4, P2, K4, BPC, K 20.
Row 31: P 19, BPC, P5, K2, P5, FPC, P 19.
Row 32: K 18, FPC, K6, P2, K6, BPC, K 18.
Row 33: P 17, BPC, P7, K2, P7, FPC, P 17.
Row 34: K 16, FPC, K8, P2, K8, BPC, K 16.
Row 35: P 15, BPC, P9, K2, P9, FPC, P 15.
Row 36: K 12, P1, (K2, P1) twice, K7, P2, K7, P1, (K2, P1) twice, K 12.
Row 37: P 12, FPC, P1, K1, P1, BPC, P7, K2, P7, FPC, P1, K1, P1, BPC, P 12.
Row 38: K 13, P1, (K1, P1) twice, K8, P2, K8, P1, (K1, P1) twice, K 13.
Row 39: P 13, FPC, K1, BPC, P8, K2, P8, FPC, K1, BPC, P 13.
Row 40: K 14, P3, K9, P2, K9, P3, K 14.
Note: Make One **(abbreviated M1)** as follows: Insert left needle under horizontal strand before next st **(Fig. 10)**, then purl into the **back** of the strand.

Fig. 10

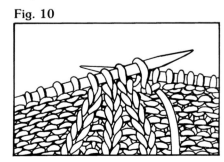

Row 41: P 14, M1, slip 1 as if to **knit**, K2 tog, PSSO, M1, P9, K2, P9, M1, slip 1 as if to **knit**, K2 tog, PSSO, M1, P 14.
Row 42: K 15, P1, K 10, P2, K 10, P1, K 15.
Row 43: P 21, work Bobble, P4, K2, P4, work Bobble, P 21.
Row 44: K 21, P1 tbl, K4, P2, K4, P1 tbl, K 21.
Row 45: P 21, FPC, P3, K2, P3, BPC, P 21.
Row 46: K 22, BPC, K2, P2, K2, FPC, K 22.
Row 47: P 23, FPC, P1, K2, P1, BPC, P 23.
Row 48: K 24, BPC, P2, FPC, K 24.
Row 49: P 25, FPC, BPC, P 25.
Row 50: K 26, P2, K 26.
Row 51: P 26, FKC, P 26.
Row 52: K 25, FPC, BPC, K 25.
Row 53: P 24, BPC, P2, FPC, P 24.
Row 54: K 23, FPC, K4, BPC, K 23.
Row 55: P 23, K1, P6, K1, P 23.
Row 56: K 23, P1, K6, P1, K 23.
Row 57: P 23, FPC, P4, BPC, P 23.
Row 58: K 24, BPC, K2, FPC, K 24.
Row 59: P 25, FPC, BPC, P 25.
Row 60: K 26, working in front of next st on left needle, purl second st, then purl first st letting both sts drop off needle together, K 26.
Row 61: Purl across.
Row 62: Knit across.
Repeat Rows 61 and 62 until square measures approximately 12″ from cast on edge, ending by working a **knit** row.
Bind off all sts leaving last loop on needle.

Edging: Drop loop from needle, insert crochet hook in loop, do **not** turn; work 3 sc in each corner and 48 sc evenly spaced across each side **(Fig. 4, page 2)**; join with slip st to first sc, finish off.

---

30. Lace Diamond Chain

Cast on 54 sts.
Row 1 AND ALL WRONG SIDE ROWS: Purl across.
Row 2 (Right side): K 24, YO **(Fig. 1a, page 1)**, SSK **(Figs. 3a-c, page 2)**, K2, YO, SSK, K 24.
Row 4: K 22, K2 tog, YO, K1, YO, SSK, K2, YO, SSK, K 23.
Row 6: K 21, K2 tog, YO, K3, YO, SSK, K2, YO, SSK, K 22.
Row 8: K 20, K2 tog, YO, K2, K2 tog, YO, K1, YO, SSK, K2, YO, SSK, K 21.
Row 10: K 19, K2 tog, YO, K2, K2 tog, YO, K3, YO, SSK, K2, YO, SSK, K 20.
Row 12: K 21, YO, SSK, K2, YO, SSK, YO, K2 tog, YO, K2, K2 tog, YO, K2 tog, K 19.
Row 14: K 22, YO, SSK, K2, YO, slip 1 as if to **knit**, K2 tog, PSSO, YO, K2, K2 tog, YO, K 21.
Row 16: K 23, YO, SSK, K2, YO, SSK, K1, K2 tog, YO, K 22.
Repeat Rows 1-16 until square measures approximately 12″ from cast on edge, ending by working a **purl** row.
Bind off all sts leaving last loop on needle.
Edging: Drop loop from needle, insert crochet hook in loop, do **not** turn; work 3 sc in each corner and 48 sc evenly spaced across each side **(Fig. 4, page 2)**; join with slip st to first sc, finish off.

31. Quatrefoil Eyelet

Cast on 56 sts.
Row 1 AND ALL WRONG SIDE ROWS: Purl across.
Row 2 (Right side): Knit across.
Row 4: K3, YO *(Fig. 1a, page 1)*, SSK *(Figs. 3a-c, page 2)*, (K6, YO, SSK) 6 times, K3.
Row 6: K1, K2 tog, YO, K1, YO, SSK, (K3, K2 tog, YO, K1, YO, SSK) 6 times, K2.
Row 8: K3, YO, SSK, (K6, YO, SSK) 6 times, K3.
Row 10: Knit across.
Row 12: K7, YO, SSK, (K6, YO, SSK) 5 times, K7.
Row 14: K5, K2 tog, YO, K1, YO, SSK, (K3, K2 tog, YO, K1, YO, SSK) 5 times, K6.
Row 16: K7, YO, SSK, (K6, YO, SSK) 5 times, K7.
Repeat Rows 1-16 until square measures approximately 12" from cast on edge, ending by working Row 10.
Bind off all sts leaving last loop on needle.
Edging: Drop loop from needle, insert crochet hook in loop, turn; work 3 sc in each corner and 48 sc evenly spaced across each side *(Fig. 4, page 2)*; join with slip st to first sc, finish off.

---

32. Yarn Over Cable

Cast on 82 sts.
Row 1 (Right side): P2, ★ slip 1 as if to **knit**, K2, PSSO, P2; repeat from ★ across: 66 sts.
Row 2: K2, ★ P1, YO *(Fig. 1d, page 1)*, P1, K2; repeat from ★ across: 82 sts.
Row 3: P2, (K3, P2) across.
Row 4: K2, (P3, K2) across.
Repeat Rows 1-4 until square measures approximately 12" from cast on edge, ending by working a **wrong** side row.
Bind off all sts leaving last loop on needle.

Edging: Drop loop from needle, insert crochet hook in loop, do **not** turn; work 3 sc in each corner and 48 sc evenly spaced across each side *(Fig. 4, page 2)*; join with slip st to first sc, finish off.

---

33. Zig Zag Stitch

Cast on 54 sts.
Row 1 (Right side): K4, slip 1 as if to **knit**, K1, YO *(Fig. 1a, page 1)*, pass the slipped st over **both** the knit st **and** the YO, ★ K2, slip 1 as if to **knit**, K1, YO, pass the slipped st over **both** the knit st **and** the YO; repeat from ★ across to last 4 sts, K4.
Row 2: Purl across.
Repeat Rows 1 and 2 until square measures approximately 12" from cast on edge, ending by working Row 1.
Bind off all sts leaving last loop on needle.
Edging: Drop loop from needle, insert crochet hook in loop, turn; work 3 sc in each corner and 48 sc evenly spaced across each side *(Fig. 4, page 2)*; join with slip st to first sc, finish off.

34. Pinnacle Chevron

Cast on 73 sts.
Row 1: P1, ★ (K2, P2) twice, K1, (P2, K2) twice, P1; repeat from ★ across.
Row 2 (Right side): K1, ★ (P2, K2) twice, P1, (K2, P2) twice, K1; repeat from ★ across.
Rows 3 and 4: Repeat Rows 1 and 2.
Row 5: P2, (K2, P2, K2, P3) 7 times, (K2, P2) twice.
Row 6: K2, (P2, K2, P2, K3) 7 times, (P2, K2) twice.
Rows 7 and 8: Repeat Rows 5 and 6.
Row 9: Repeat Row 2.
Rows 10-12: Repeat Rows 1 and 2 once, then repeat Row 1 once **more**.
Row 13: Repeat Row 6.
Rows 14-16: Repeat Rows 5 and 6 once, then repeat Row 5 once **more**.
Repeat Rows 1-16 until square measures approximately 12" from cast on edge, ending by working a **right** side row.
Bind off all sts leaving last loop on needle.
Edging: Drop loop from needle, insert crochet hook in loop, turn; work 3 sc in each corner and 48 sc evenly spaced across each side *(Fig. 4, page 2)*; join with slip st to first sc, finish off.

---

35. Elfin Lace

Cast on 57 sts.
Row 1 AND ALL WRONG SIDE ROWS: Purl across.
Row 2: K2, YO *(Fig. 1a, page 1)*, SSK *(Figs. 3a-c, page 2)*, (K6, YO, SSK) 6 times, K5.
Row 4: K3, YO, SSK, (K3, K2 tog, YO, K1, YO, SSK) 6 times, K4.
Row 6: K4, YO, SSK, (K1, K2 tog, YO, K3, YO, SSK) 6 times, K3.
Row 8: K2, K2 tog, YO, K5, (YO, slip 2 as if to **knit**, K1, P2SSO, YO, K5) 6 times.
Row 10: (K6, YO, SSK) 7 times, K1.
Row 12: K4, K2 tog, YO, (K1, YO, SSK, K3, K2 tog, YO) 6 times, K3.
Row 14: K3, K2 tog, YO, (K3, YO, SSK, K1, K2 tog, YO) 6 times, K4.
Row 16: K5, YO, (slip 2 as if to **knit**, K1, P2SSO, YO, K5, YO) 6 times, K2 tog, K2.
Repeat Rows 1-16 until square measures approximately 12" from cast on edge, ending by working a **purl** row.
Bind off all sts leaving last loop on needle.
Edging: Drop loop from needle, insert crochet hook in loop, do **not** turn; work 3 sc in each corner and 48 sc evenly spaced across each side *(Fig. 4, page 2)*; join with slip st to first sc, finish off.

36. Fancy Lozenge Pattern

Cast on 56 sts.
Row 1: (Right side): K2, (P4, K2, P2, K4, P4, K2) 3 times.
Row 2: P3, K4, P2, K2, P2, K4, (P4, K4, P2, K2, P2, K4) twice, P1, K1, P1.
Row 3: P2, K2, P4, K4, P4, (K2, P2, K2, P4, K4, P4) twice, K4.
Row 4: P1, (K2, P2, K4, P2, K4, P4) 3 times, K1.
Row 5: K2, P2, K2, P8, K2, ★ (P2, K2) twice, P8, K2; repeat from ★ once **more**, P2, K2.
Row 6: K1, P2, K2, P2, K6, P4, ★ (K2, P2) twice, K6, P4; repeat from ★ once **more**, K2, P1.
Row 7: (P2, K2) twice, P4, K2, ★ (P2, K2) 3 times, P4, K2; repeat from ★ once **more**, P2, K2, P2.
Row 8: P1, K2, P4, K6, ★ (P2, K2) twice, P4, K6; repeat from ★ once **more**, P2, K2, P2, K1.
Row 9: K2, P2, K2, P8, K2, ★ (P2, K2) twice, P8, K2; repeat from ★ once **more**, P3, K1.
Row 10: K1, (P4, K4, P2, K4, P2, K2) 3 times, P1.
Row 11: P2, K2, P4, K4, P4, (K2, P2, K2, P4, K4, P4) twice, K4.
Row 12: P3, K4, P2, K2, P2, K4, (P4, K4, P2, K2, P2, K4) twice, P3.
Row 13: K2, (P4, K4, P2, K2, P4, K2) across.
Row 14: K5, P2, (K2, P2) twice, ★ K8, P2, (K2, P2) twice; repeat from ★ once **more**, K5.
Row 15: P4, K4, (P2, K2) twice, ★ P6, K4, (P2, K2) twice; repeat from ★ once **more**, P4.
Row 16: K3, P2, (K2, P2) 3 times, ★ K4, P2, (K2, P2) 3 times; repeat from ★ once **more**, K3.
Row 17: P4, (K2, P2) twice, K4, ★ P6, (K2, P2) twice, K4; repeat from ★ once **more**, P4.
Row 18: K5, P2, (K2, P2) twice, ★ K8, P2, (K2, P2) twice; repeat from ★ once **more**, K5.
Repeat Rows 1-18 until square measures approximately 12″ from cast on edge, ending by working a **right** side row.
Bind off all sts leaving last loop on needle.
Edging: Drop loop from needle, insert crochet hook in loop, turn; work 3 sc in each corner and 48 sc evenly spaced across each side *(Fig. 4, page 2)*; join with slip st to first sc, finish off.

---

37. Reverse Herringbone Faggot

Cast on 57 sts.
Row 1: K2, P4, (K3, P4) 7 times, K2.
Row 2 (Right side): P2, K2 tog, YO *(Fig. 1a, page 1)*, K2, (P3, K2 tog, YO, K2) 7 times, P2.
Row 3: K2, P2 tog, YO *(Fig. 1d, page 1)*, P2, (K3, P2 tog, YO, P2) 7 times, K2.
Repeat Rows 2 and 3 until square measures approximately 12″ from cast on edge, ending by working Row 2.
Bind off all sts leaving last loop on needle.
Edging: Drop loop from needle, insert crochet hook in loop, turn; work 3 sc in each corner and 48 sc evenly spaced across each side *(Fig. 4, page 2)*; join with slip st to first sc, finish off.

---

38. Moss and Rib Block Stitch

Cast on 67 sts.
Row 1 (Right side): K3, P1, K3, ★ P2, K1, P2, K3, P1, K3; repeat from ★ across.
Row 2: P3, K1, P3, ★ K2, P1, K2, P3, K1, P3; repeat from ★ across.
Row 3: K2, P1, K1, P1, K2, ★ P2, K1, P2, K2, P1, K1, P1, K2; repeat from ★ across.
Row 4: P2, K1, P1, K1, P2, ★ K2, P1, K2, P2, K1, P1, K1, P2; repeat from ★ across.
Row 5: K1, (P1, K1) 3 times, ★ (P2, K1) twice, (P1, K1) 3 times; repeat from ★ across.
Row 6: P1, (K1, P1) 3 times, ★ (K2, P1) twice, (K1, P1) 3 times; repeat from ★ across.
Rows 7 and 8: Repeat Rows 3 and 4.
Rows 9 and 10: Repeat Rows 1 and 2.
Row 11: (K1, P2) twice, ★ K3, P1, K3, P2, K1, P2; repeat from ★ across to last st, K1.
Row 12: (P1, K2) twice, ★ P3, K1, P3, K2, P1, K2; repeat from ★ across to last st, P1.
Row 13: (K1, P2) twice, ★ K2, P1, K1, P1, K2, P2, K1, P2; repeat from ★ across to last st, K1.
Row 14: (P1, K2) twice, ★ P2, K1, P1, K1, P2, K2, P1, K2; repeat from ★ across to last st, P1.
Row 15: (K1, P2) twice, ★ (K1, P1) 3 times, (K1, P2) twice; repeat from ★ across to last st, K1.
Row 16: (P1, K2) twice, ★ (P1, K1) 3 times, (P1, K2) twice; repeat from ★ across to last st, P1.
Rows 17 and 18: Repeat Rows 13 and 14.
Rows 19 and 20: Repeat Rows 11 and 12.
Repeat Rows 1-20 until square measures approximately 12″ from cast on edge, ending by working a **right** side row.
Bind off all sts leaving last loop on needle.
Edging: Drop loop from needle, insert crochet hook in loop, turn; work 3 sc in each corner and 48 sc evenly spaced across each side *(Fig. 4, page 2)*; join with slip st to first sc, finish off.

---

39. Ribbed Cables

Additional materials: Cable needle

Cast on 80 sts.
Row 1: K4, P2, (K2, P1, K2, P2) 10 times, K4.
Row 2 (Right side): P4, K2, (P2, K1, P2, K2) 10 times, P4.
Row 3: K4, P2, (K2, P1, K2, P2) 10 times, K4.
Row 4: P4, work Right Twist as follows: knit second st on left needle, then knit the first st letting both sts drop off needle together **(Right Twist made)**, ★ P2, K1, P2, K2, P2, K1, P2, work Right Twist; repeat from ★ 4 times **more**, P4.
Rows 5-11: Repeat Rows 1-4 once, then repeat Rows 1-3 once **more**.
Row 12: P4, work Right Twist, ★ P2, slip 4 sts onto cable needle and hold in **back** of work, (K1, P2, K1) from left needle, (K1, P2, K1) from cable needle, P2, work Right Twist; repeat from ★ 4 times **more**, P4.
Repeat Rows 1-12 until square measures approximately 12″ from cast on edge, ending by working Row 1 or Row 9.
Bind off all sts leaving last loop on needle.
Edging: Drop loop from needle, insert crochet hook in loop, do **not** turn; work 3 sc in each corner and 48 sc evenly spaced across each side *(Fig. 4, page 2)*; join with slip st to first sc, finish off.

40. Flame Chevron

Cast on 57 sts.
Rows 1-6: K1, (P1, K1) across.
Row 7 (Right side): (K1, P1) twice, ★ SSK (**Figs. 3a-c, page 2**), K5, YO (**Figs. 1a & c, page 1**); repeat from ★ across to last 4 sts, (P1, K1) twice.
Row 8 AND ALL WRONG SIDE ROWS: K1, P1, K1, purl across to last 3 sts, K1, P1, K1.
Row 9: (K1, P1) twice, ★ SSK, K4, YO, K1; repeat from ★ across to last 4 sts, (P1, K1) twice.
Row 11: (K1, P1) twice, ★ SSK, K3, YO, K2; repeat from ★ across to last 4 sts, (P1, K1) twice.
Row 13: (K1, P1) twice, ★ SSK, K2, YO, K3; repeat from ★ across to last 4 sts, (P1, K1) twice.
Row 15: (K1, P1) twice, ★ SSK, K1, YO, K4; repeat from ★ across to last 4 sts, (P1, K1) twice.
Row 17: (K1, P1) twice, ★ SSK, YO, K5; repeat from ★ across to last 4 sts, (P1, K1) twice.
Row 19: (K1, P1) twice, ★ K5, K2 tog, YO; repeat from ★ across to last 4 sts, (P1, K1) twice.
Row 21: (K1, P1) twice, ★ K4, K2 tog, K1, YO; repeat from ★ across to last 4 sts, (P1, K1) twice.
Row 23: (K1, P1) twice, ★ K3, K2 tog, K2, YO; repeat from ★ across to last 4 sts, (P1, K1) twice.
Row 25: (K1, P1) twice, ★ K2, K2 tog, K3, YO; repeat from ★ across to last 4 sts, (P1, K1) twice.
Row 27: (K1, P1) twice, ★ K1, K2 tog, K4, YO; repeat from ★ across to last 4 sts, (P1, K1) twice.
Row 29: (K1, P1) twice, ★ K2 tog, K5, YO; repeat from ★ across to last 4 sts, (P1, K1) twice.
Row 31: (K1, P1) twice, ★ SSK, K5, YO; repeat from ★ across to last 4 sts, (P1, K1) twice.
Rows 32-71: Repeat Rows 8-31 once, then repeat Rows 8-23 once **more**.
Rows 72-77: K1, (P1, K1) across.
Bind off all sts leaving last loop on needle.
Edging: Drop loop from needle, insert crochet hook in loop, turn; work 3 sc in each corner and 48 sc evenly spaced across each side (**Fig. 4, page 2**); join with slip st to first sc, finish off.

---

41. Lizard Lattice

Cast on 57 sts.
Row 1 (Right side): Knit across.
Row 2: Purl across.
Rows 3 and 4: Repeat Rows 1 and 2.
Row 5: P3, (K3, P3) across.
Row 6: Purl across.
Rows 7-10: Repeat Rows 5 and 6 twice.
Rows 11-13: Repeat Rows 1-3.
Row 14: P3, (K3, P3) across.
Row 15: Knit across.
Rows 16-18: Repeat Rows 14 and 15 once, then repeat Row 14 once **more**.
Repeat Rows 1-18 until square measures approximately 12" from cast on edge, ending by working Row 13.
Bind off all sts leaving last loop on needle.
Edging: Drop loop from needle, insert crochet hook in loop, turn; work 3 sc in each corner and 48 sc evenly spaced across each side (**Fig. 4, page 2**); join with slip st to first sc, finish off.

42. Double Twisted Rib

Left Twist (abbreviated LT): Working behind first st on left needle, knit into the back of the second st, then knit the first st letting both sts drop off needle together.
Right Twist (abbreviated RT): Knit second st on left needle, then knit the first st letting both sts drop off needle together.

Cast on 68 sts.
Row 1 (Right side): P2, (LT, RT, P2) across.
Row 2: K2, (P4, K2) across.
Repeat Rows 1 and 2 until square measures approximately 12" from cast on edge, ending by working Row 2.
Bind off all sts leaving last loop on needle.
Edging: Drop loop from needle, insert crochet hook in loop, do **not** turn; work 3 sc in each corner and 48 sc evenly spaced across each side (**Fig. 4, page 2**); join with slip st to first sc, finish off.

---

43. Staghorn Cable

Additional materials: Cable needle

Back Cable (abbreviated BC): Slip 2 sts onto cable needle and hold in **back** of work, K2, K2 from cable needle.
Front Cable (abbreviated FC): Slip 2 sts onto cable needle and hold in **front** of work, K2, K2 from cable needle.
Cable: Slip 1 st onto cable needle and hold in **front** of work, K2, K1 from cable needle.

Cast on 86 sts.
Row 1 AND ALL WRONG SIDE ROWS: P1, K1, (P3, K2) twice, P 16, ★ K2, P3, K2, P 16; repeat from ★ once **more**, (K2, P3) twice, K1, P1.
Row 2 (Right side): K1, P1, (K3, P2) twice, K4, BC, FC, K4, ★ P2, K3, P2, K4, BC, FC, K4; repeat from ★ once **more**, (P2, K3) twice, P1, K1.
Row 4: K1, P1, (work Cable, P2) twice, K2, BC, K4, FC, K2, ★ P2, work Cable, P2, K2, BC, K4, FC, K2; repeat from ★ once **more**, (P2, work Cable) twice, P1, K1.
Row 6: K1, P1, (K3, P2) twice, BC, K8, FC, ★ P2, K3, P2, BC, K8, FC; repeat from ★ once **more**, (P2, K3) twice, P1, K1.
Row 8: K1, P1, (work Cable, P2) twice, K4, BC, FC, K4, ★ P2, work Cable, P2, K4, BC, FC, K4; repeat from ★ once **more**, (P2, work Cable) twice, P1, K1.
Row 10: K1, P1, (K3, P2) twice, K2, BC, K4, FC, K2, ★ P2, K3, P2, K2, BC, K4, FC, K2; repeat from ★ once **more**, (P2, K3) twice, P1, K1.
Row 12: K1, P1, (work Cable, P2) twice, BC, K8, FC, ★ P2, work Cable, P2, BC, K8, FC; repeat from ★ once **more**, (P2, work Cable) twice, P1, K1.
Repeat Rows 1-12 until square measures approximately 12" from cast on edge, ending by working a **right** side row.
Bind off all sts leaving last loop on needle.
Edging: Drop loop from needle, insert crochet hook in loop, turn; work 3 sc in each corner and 48 sc evenly spaced across each side (**Fig. 4, page 2**); join with slip st to first sc, finish off.

44. Hourglass Cable and Bobbles

Additional materials: Cable needle

Bobble: (K, P, K, P, K) **all** in next st, **turn**, K5, **turn**, P5, slip second, third, fourth and fifth sts on right needle over first st.
Back Cable (abbreviated BC): Slip 1 st onto cable needle and hold in **back** of work, K1 tbl, P1 from cable needle.
Front Cable (abbreviated FC): Slip 1 st onto cable needle and hold in **front** of work, P1, K1 tbl from cable needle.

Cast on 75 sts.
Row 1 (Right side): P1, K1 tbl, (P3, K1 tbl) twice, P4, K1 tbl, P1, K1 tbl 3 times, P1, K1 tbl, P4, K1 tbl, ★ P3, K1 tbl, P4, K1 tbl, P1, K1 tbl 3 times, P1, K1 tbl, P4, K1 tbl; repeat from ★ once **more**, (P3, K1 tbl) twice, P1.
Row 2: K1, P1 tbl, (K3, P1 tbl) twice, K4, P1 tbl, K1, P1 tbl 3 times, K1, P1 tbl, K4, P1 tbl, ★ K3, P1 tbl, K4, P1 tbl, K1, P1 tbl 3 times, K1, P1 tbl, K4, P1 tbl; repeat from ★ once **more**, (K3, P1 tbl) twice, K1.
Row 3: P1, K1 tbl, (P1, work Bobble, P1, K1 tbl) twice, P3, BC twice, K1 tbl, FC twice, P3, K1 tbl, P1, ★ work Bobble, P1, K1 tbl, P3, BC twice, K1 tbl, FC twice, P3, K1 tbl, P1; repeat from ★ once **more**, (work Bobble, P1, K1 tbl, P1) twice.
Row 4: K1, P1 tbl, (K3, P1 tbl) 3 times, ★ (K1, P1 tbl) 4 times, (K3, P1 tbl) 3 times; repeat from ★ 2 times **more**, K1.
Row 5: P1, K1 tbl, (P3, K1 tbl) twice, P2, BC twice, P1, K1 tbl, P1, FC twice, P2, K1 tbl, ★ P3, K1 tbl, P2, BC twice, P1, K1 tbl, P1, FC twice, P2, K1 tbl; repeat from ★ once **more**, (P3, K1 tbl) twice, P1.
Row 6: K1, P1 tbl, (K3, P1 tbl) twice, K2, P1 tbl, K1, P1 tbl, (K2, P1 tbl) twice, K1, P1 tbl, K2, P1 tbl, ★ K3, P1 tbl, K2, P1 tbl, K1, P1 tbl, (K2, P1 tbl) twice, K1, P1 tbl, K2, P1 tbl; repeat from ★ once **more**, (K3, P1 tbl) twice, K1.
Row 7: P1, K1 tbl, (P1, work Bobble, P1, K1 tbl) twice, P1, BC twice, P2, K1 tbl, P2, FC twice, P1, K1 tbl, P1, ★ work Bobble, P1, K1 tbl, P1, BC twice, P2, K1 tbl, P2, FC twice, P1, K1 tbl, P1; repeat from ★ once **more**, (work Bobble, P1, K1 tbl, P1) twice.
Row 8: K1, P1 tbl, (K3, P1 tbl) twice, (K1, P1 tbl) twice, K3, P1 tbl, K3, P1 tbl, (K1, P1 tbl) twice, ★ K3, P1 tbl, (K1, P1 tbl) twice, (K3, P1 tbl) twice, (K1, P1 tbl) twice; repeat from ★ once **more**, (K3, P1 tbl) twice, K1.
Row 9: P1, K1 tbl, (P3, K1 tbl) twice, BC twice, P3, K1 tbl, P3, FC twice, K1 tbl, ★ P3, K1 tbl, BC twice, P3, K1 tbl, P3, FC twice, K1 tbl; repeat from ★ once **more**, (P3, K1 tbl) twice, P1.
Row 10: K1, (P1 tbl, K3) twice, P1 tbl twice, K1, P1 tbl, (K4, P1 tbl) twice, K1, P1 tbl twice, ★ K3, P1 tbl twice, K1, P1 tbl, (K4, P1 tbl) twice, K1, P1 tbl twice; repeat from ★ once **more**, (K3, P1 tbl) twice, K1.
Row 11: P1, K1 tbl, (P1, work Bobble, P1, K1 tbl) twice, FC twice, P3, K1 tbl, P3, BC twice, K1 tbl, P1, ★ work Bobble, P1, K1 tbl, FC twice, P3, K1 tbl, P3, BC twice, K1 tbl, P1; repeat from ★ once **more**, (work Bobble, P1, K1 tbl, P1) twice.
Row 12: K1, P1 tbl, (K3, P1 tbl) twice, (K1, P1 tbl) twice, (K3, P1 tbl) twice, (K1, P1 tbl) twice, ★ K3, P1 tbl, (K1, P1 tbl) twice, (K3, P1 tbl) twice, (K1, P1 tbl) twice; repeat from ★ once **more**, (K3, P1 tbl) twice, K1.
Row 13: P1, K1 tbl, (P3, K1 tbl) twice, P1, FC twice, P2, K1 tbl, P2, BC twice, P1, K1 tbl, ★ P3, K1 tbl, P1, FC twice, P2, K1 tbl, P2, BC twice, P1, K1 tbl; repeat from ★ once **more**, (P3, K1 tbl) twice, P1.
Row 14: K1, P1 tbl, (K3, P1 tbl) twice, K2, P1 tbl, K1, P1 tbl, (K2, P1 tbl) twice, K1, P1 tbl, K2, P1 tbl, ★ K3, P1 tbl, K2, P1 tbl, K1, P1 tbl, (K2, P1 tbl) twice, K1, P1 tbl, K2, P1 tbl; repeat from ★ once **more**, (K3, P1 tbl) twice, K1.
Row 15: P1, K1 tbl, (P1, work Bobble, P1, K1 tbl) twice, P2, FC twice, P1, K1 tbl, P1, BC twice, P2, K1 tbl, P1, ★ work Bobble, P1, K1 tbl, P2, FC twice, P1, K1 tbl, P1, BC twice, P2, K1 tbl, P1; repeat from ★ once **more**, (work Bobble, P1, K1 tbl, P1) twice.
Row 16: K1, P1 tbl, (K3, P1 tbl) 3 times, ★ (K1, P1 tbl) 4 times, (K3, P1 tbl) 3 times; repeat from ★ 2 times **more**, K1.
Row 17: P1, (K1 tbl, P3) 3 times, ★ FC twice, K1 tbl, BC twice, P3, (K1 tbl, P3) twice; repeat from ★ 2 times **more**, K1 tbl, P1.
Repeat Rows 2-17 until square measures approximately 12" from cast on edge, ending by working Row 17.
Bind off all sts leaving last loop on needle.

Edging: Drop loop from needle, insert crochet hook in loop, turn; work 3 sc in each corner and 48 sc evenly spaced across each side **(Fig. 4, page 2)**; join with slip st to first sc, finish off.

---

45. Little Tent Stitch

Note: When instructed to slip 5 stitches, always slip as if to **purl** with yarn held **loosely** in front .

Cast on 57 sts.
Row 1: K2, P5, (K3, P5) 6 times, K2.
Row 2 (Right side): K2, slip 5, (K3, slip 5) 6 times, K2.
Row 3: K2, P5, (K3, P5) 6 times, K2.
Row 4: K4, K1 under strand **(Fig. 2, page 2)**, (K7, K1 under strand) 6 times, K4.
Repeat Rows 1-4 until square measures approximately 12" from cast on edge, ending by working Row 4.
Bind off all sts leaving last loop on needle.

Edging: Drop loop from needle, insert crochet hook in loop, turn; work 3 sc in each corner and 48 sc evenly spaced across each side **(Fig. 4, page 2)**; join with slip st to first sc, finish off.

---

46. Basketweave

Cast on 56 sts.
Row 1 (Right side): Knit across.
Row 2: (K5, P3) across.
Row 3: (K3, P5) across.
Row 4: (K5, P3) across.
Row 5: Knit across.
Row 6: (P5, K3) across.
Row 7: (P3, K5) across.
Row 8: (P5, K3) across.
Repeat Rows 1-8 until square measures approximately 12" from cast on edge, ending by working a **right** side row.
Bind off all sts leaving last loop on needle.

Edging: Drop loop from needle, insert crochet hook in loop, turn; work 3 sc in each corner and 48 sc evenly spaced across each side **(Fig. 4, page 2)**; join with slip st to first sc, finish off.

47. Checkered Fleurette

Cast on 55 sts.
Row 1 AND ALL WRONG SIDE ROWS: Purl across.
Row 2 (Right side): K7, ★ P2 tog, YO *(Fig. 1b, page 1)*, K1, YO *(Fig. 1c, page 1)*, P2 tog, K7; repeat from ★ across.
Row 4: K7, ★ YO, P2 tog, K1, P2 tog, YO, K7; repeat from ★ across.
Row 6: Repeat Row 4.
Row 8: K7, ★ P2 tog, YO, K1, YO, P2 tog, K7; repeat from ★ across.
Row 10: K4, YO, P2 tog, K7, P2 tog, YO, ★ K1, YO, P2 tog, K7, P2 tog, YO; repeat from ★ 2 times **more**, K4.
Row 12: K4, P2 tog, YO, K7, YO, P2 tog, ★ K1, P2 tog, YO, K7, YO, P2 tog; repeat from ★ 2 times **more**, K4.
Row 14: Repeat Row 12.
Row 16: Repeat Row 10.
Repeat Rows 1-16 until square measures approximately 12″ from cast on edge, ending by working a **purl** row.
Bind off all sts leaving last loop on needle.
Edging: Drop loop from needle, insert crochet hook in loop, do **not** turn; work 3 sc in each corner and 48 sc evenly spaced across each side *(Fig. 4, page 2)*; join with slip st to first sc, finish off.

48. Daisy Stitch

Cast on 55 sts.
Rows 1-6: Beginning with a **knit** row, work in Stockinette Stitch.
Note: Work Daisy St as follows:
Insert right needle in st 3 rows **below** second st on left needle *(Fig. 11a)* and pull up a loop, (K2, pull up a loop in same st as first loop) twice **(Daisy St made, Fig. 11b)**.

Fig. 11a   **Fig. 11b**

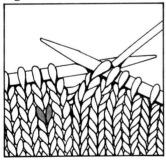 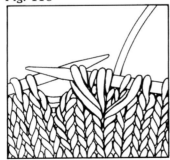

Row 7 (Right side): (K6, work Daisy St) 5 times, K5: 70 sts.
Row 8: ★ P5, P2 tog, (P1, P2 tog) twice; repeat from ★ 4 times **more**, P5: 55 sts.
Rows 9-14: Work in Stockinette Stitch.
Row 15: K 11, work Daisy St, (K6, work Daisy St) 3 times, K 10: 67 sts.
Row 16: P 10, P2 tog, (P1, P2 tog) twice, ★ P5, P2 tog, (P1, P2 tog) twice; repeat from ★ 2 times **more**, P 10: 55 sts.
Repeat Rows 1-16 until square measures approximately 12″ from cast on edge, ending by working a **wrong** side row.
Bind off all sts leaving last loop on needle.
Edging: Drop loop from needle, insert crochet hook in loop, do **not** turn; work 3 sc in each corner and 48 sc evenly spaced across each side *(Fig. 4, page 2)*; join with slip st to first sc, finish off.

49. Quilted Lattice

Note: When instructed to slip stitches, always slip as if to **purl**, with yarn held **loosely** in front.

Cast on 55 sts.
Row 1 AND ALL WRONG SIDE ROWS: Purl across.
Row 2: K4, slip 5, (K1, slip 5) 7 times, K4.
Row 4: K6, K1 under strand *(Fig. 2, page 2)*, (K5, K1 under strand) 7 times, K6.
Row 6: K3, slip 3, K1, (slip 5, K1) 7 times, slip 3, K3.
Row 8: K3, K1 under strand, (K5, K1 under strand) 8 times, K3.
Repeat Rows 1-8 until square measures approximately 12″ from cast on edge, ending by working Row 1 or Row 5.
Bind off all sts leaving last loop on needle.
Edging: Drop loop from needle, insert crochet hook in loop, do **not** turn; work 3 sc in each corner and 48 sc evenly spaced across each side *(Fig. 4, page 2)*; join with slip st to first sc, finish off.

50. Small Wheatear Cable

Additional materials: Cable needle

Cast on 80 sts.
Row 1: K3, (P8, K3) across.
Row 2 (Right side): P1, K1, P1, ★ slip 2 sts onto cable needle and hold in **back** of work, K2, K2 from cable needle, slip 2 sts onto cable needle and hold in **front** of work, K2, K2 from cable needle, P1, K1, P1; repeat from ★ across.
Row 3: K3, (P8, K3) across.
Row 4: P1, K1, P1, (K8, P1, K1, P1) across.
Repeat Rows 1-4 until square measures approximately 12″ from cast on edge, ending by working Row 2.
Bind off all sts leaving last loop on needle.
Edging: Drop loop from needle, insert crochet hook in loop, turn; work 3 sc in each corner and 48 sc evenly spaced across each side *(Fig. 4, page 2)*; join with slip st to first sc, finish off.

51. Reversible Garter Stitch Rib

Cast on 56 sts.
Row 1: (K2, P2) across.
Row 2: Knit across.
Repeat Rows 1 and 2 until square measures approximately 12″ from cast on edge, ending by working Row 2.
Bind off all sts leaving last loop on needle.
Edging: Drop loop from needle, insert crochet hook in loop, turn; work 3 sc in each corner and 48 sc evenly spaced across each side *(Fig. 4, page 2)*; join with slip st to first sc, finish off.

52. Shadow Cable

Additional materials: *Cable needle*

Back Cable (abbreviated BC): Slip 2 sts onto cable needle and hold in **back** of work, K2, K2 from cable needle.
Front Cable (abbreviated FC): Slip 2 sts onto cable needle and hold in **front** of work, K2, K2 from cable needle.

Cast on 54 sts.
Row 1: Purl across.
Row 2 (Right side): Knit across.
Row 3: Purl across increasing 12 sts evenly spaced: 66 sts.
Row 4: K1, BC, (K4, BC) 7 times, K5.
Row 5 AND ALL WRONG SIDE ROWS: Purl across.
Row 6: Knit across.
Row 8: K5, FC, (K4, FC) 7 times, K1.
Row 10: Knit across.
Row 12: K1, BC, (K4, BC) 7 times, K5.
Repeat Rows 5-12 until square measures approximately 11½″ from cast on edge, ending by working a **right** side row.
Next Row: Purl across decreasing 12 sts evenly spaced: 54 sts.
Last 2 Rows: Work in Stockinette Stitch.
Bind off all sts leaving last loop on needle.

Edging: Drop loop from needle, insert crochet hook in loop, do **not** turn; work 3 sc in each corner and 48 sc evenly spaced across each side *(Fig. 4, page 2)*; join with slip st to first sc, finish off.

---

53. King Charles Brocade

Cast on 54 sts.
Row 1 (Right side): K4, P1, K1, ★ P1, K9, P1, K1; repeat from ★ across.
Row 2: K1, P1, K1, ★ P7, K1, (P1, K1) twice; repeat from ★ 3 times **more**, P3.
Row 3: K2, ★ P1, (K1, P1) 3 times, K5; repeat from ★ 3 times **more**, (P1, K1) twice.
Row 4: P2, K1, P1, K1, ★ P3, K1, P1, K1; repeat from ★ 7 times **more**, P1.
Row 5: P1, K1, P1, ★ K5, P1, (K1, P1) 3 times; repeat from ★ 3 times **more**, K3.
Row 6: P4, ★ K1, (P1, K1) twice, P7; repeat from ★ 3 times **more**, K1, P1.
Row 7: P1, ★ K9, P1, K1, P1; repeat from ★ 3 times **more**, K5.
Row 8: Repeat Row 6.
Row 9: Repeat Row 5.
Row 10: Repeat Row 4.
Row 11: Repeat Row 3.
Row 12: Repeat Row 2.
Repeat Rows 1-12 until square measures approximately 12″ from cast on edge, ending by working a **right** side row.
Bind off all sts leaving last loop on needle.

Edging: Drop loop from needle, insert crochet hook in loop, turn; work 3 sc in each corner and 48 sc evenly spaced across each side *(Fig. 4, page 2)*; join with slip st to first sc, finish off.

---

54. Turtle Check

Additional materials: *Cable needle*

Left Twist 4 (abbreviated LT4): Slip 1 st onto cable needle and hold in **front** of work, P3, K1 from cable needle.
Right Twist 4 (abbreviated RT4): Slip 3 sts onto cable needle and hold in **back** of work, K1, P3 from cable needle.

Cast on 54 sts.
Rows 1-6: Knit across.
Row 7: Knit across increasing 6 sts evenly spaced: 60 sts.
Row 8 (Right side): K9, P6, (K6, P6) 3 times, K9.
Row 9: K5, P4, K6, (P6, K6) 3 times, P4, K5.
Row 10: K8, LT4, RT4, (K4, LT4, RT4) 3 times, K8.
Row 11: K5, P3, K3, P2, K3, (P4, K3, P2, K3) 3 times, P3, K5.
Row 12: K7, LT4, K2, RT4, (K2, LT4, K2, RT4) 3 times, K7.
Row 13: K5, P2, K3, P4, K3, P2, (K3, P4, K3, P2) 3 times, K5.
Row 14: K6, LT4, K4, RT4, (LT4, K4, RT4) 3 times, K6.
Rows 15-19: Repeat Rows 8 and 9 twice, then repeat Row 8 once **more**.
Row 20: K6, RT4, K4, LT4, (RT4, K4, LT4) 3 times, K6.
Row 21: Repeat Row 13.
Row 22: K7, RT4, K2, LT4, (K2, RT4, K2, LT4) 3 times, K7.
Row 23: Repeat Row 11.
Row 24: K8, RT4, LT4, (K4, RT4, LT4) 3 times, K8.
Row 25: Repeat Row 9.
Rows 26 and 27: Repeat Rows 8 and 9.
Repeat Rows 8-27 until square measures approximately 11″ from cast on edge, ending by working a **wrong** side row.
Next Row: Knit across decreasing 6 sts evenly spaced: 54 sts.
Last 6 Rows: Knit across.
Bind off all sts leaving last loop on needle.

Edging: Drop loop from needle, insert crochet hook in loop, turn; work 3 sc in each corner and 48 sc evenly spaced across each side *(Fig. 4, page 2)*; join with slip st to first sc, finish off.

---

55. Fancy Shell Rib

Cast on 55 sts.
Rows 1-6: Knit across.
Row 7 (Right side): K2, P2, ★ K1, [YO *(Fig. 1a, page 1)*, K1] 4 times, P2; repeat from ★ across to last 2 sts, K2: 83 sts.
Row 8: K4, P1, (K1, P1) 4 times, ★ K2, P1, (K1, P1) 4 times; repeat from ★ across to last 4 sts, K4.
Row 9: K2, P2, ★ K1, P1, SSK *(Figs. 3a-c, page 2)*, K1, K2 tog, P1, K1, P2; repeat from ★ across to last 2 sts, K2: 69 sts.
Row 10: K4, P1, K1, P3 tog, K1, P1, ★ K2, P1, K1, P3 tog, K1, P1; repeat from ★ across to last 4 sts, K4: 55 sts.
Rows 11-70: Repeat Rows 7-10, 15 times.
Rows 71-76: Knit across.
Bind off all sts leaving last loop on needle.

Edging: Drop loop from needle, insert crochet hook in loop, do **not** turn; work 3 sc in each corner and 48 sc evenly spaced across each side *(Fig. 4, page 2)*; join with slip st to first sc, finish off.